Return to Montague Island

More Mysteries and Logic Puzzles

R. Wayne Schmittberger

PUZZLE
WRIGHT
PRESS
New York

PUZZLE
WRIGHT
PRESS

New York

An Imprint of Sterling Publishing Co., Inc.
1166 Avenue of the Americas
New York, NY 10036

ISBN 978-1-4549-3393-9

Distributed in Canada by Sterling Publishing Co., Inc.
c/o Canadian Manda Group, 664 Annette Street
Toronto, Ontario M6S 2C8, Canada
Distributed in the United Kingdom by GMC Distribution Services
Castle Place, 166 High Street, Lewes, East Sussex BN7 1XU, England
Distributed in Australia by NewSouth Books
University of New South Wales, Sydney, NSW 2052, Australia

For information about custom editions, special sales, and premium and
corporate purchases, please contact Sterling Special Sales at 800-805-5489 or
specialsales@sterlingpublishing.com.

Manufactured in China

2   4   6   8   10   9   7   5   3   1

sterlingpublishing.com
puzzlewright.com

Cover image: Nido Huebl / Shutterstock.com

Contents

Introduction 4

Weekend 1 5
Return to the Island • House Rules • Key Deductions • The New Guests • Murder in the Game Alcove

Weekend 2 12
Film Festival • Bookshelf • Six, Zero • Synchronized Walking

Weekend 3 18
Murder at the Embassy • A Day of Civilization • The Memorable Mosaic

Interlude....................................24

Weekend 4 25
Three-Card Poker • Murder in the Morning • Full House • Sailing the Seven Seas

Weekend 5 32
Secret Passages • Name Games • Snark Hunting

Weekend 6 38
Regatta • Murder in the Wine Cellar • Speed Darts

Interlude....................................43

Weekend 7 44
Web of Lies • ESP Test • Shell Game • Truth Counts

Weekend 8 48
Beach Volleyball • Barbecue • Hide and Seek

Weekend 9 54
To the Lighthouse • Shooting Match • Double Dates

Interlude....................................59

Weekend 10 60
Skeletons • Just Desserts • Numbers Game

Weekend 11 65
Mini Mahjong • The Missing Medallion • Book Exchange

Weekend 12 70
Attack in the Foyer • Tropical Taste Test • Revelation

Answers and Explanations 74

Montague Island Map 17
Montague Mansion Floor Plan 33

Introduction

My idea for this book's predecessor, *Montague Island Mysteries and Other Logic Puzzles*, was to tell a story set in a world in which mysteries and logic puzzles exist naturally, much like songs in a play whose subject is the making of a musical. And so I imagined an island home of a wealthy couple who are passionate about playing games, solving puzzles, and creating puzzles for others to solve. In that book, the couple invite a group of guests to their island to act out parts in mysteries that the Montagues have created, play in game tournaments, and take part in a summer-long puzzle-solving competition.

As in the first book (not a prerequisite for this book), readers will see the island through the eyes of Taylor, a slightly mysterious person who may be a private investigator, security consultant, bodyguard, or a combination of all three. The first book never reveals whether Taylor is male or female, and the unisex name was deliberately chosen so that the reader can imagine any possibility. This time, though, Taylor's reason for being on the island is very different from what it was in the first book.

With the exception of Taylor, *Return to Montague Island* features an entirely new set of guests. The new group is generally much younger and more athletically oriented than the previous group, though no less adept at puzzle solving. There are many more additional visitors to the island this time, including seven members of a sailing club who appear in multiple puzzles.

Once again you'll find some traditional logic puzzles that can be solved with a grid, unconventional puzzles that require special methods, and mysteries in which guilty suspects may make false statements to mislead the solver. My special thanks to Francis Heaney, whose puzzle-testing and editing have greatly improved both this and the previous book.

May you enjoy your visit.

—R. Wayne Schmittberger

Return to the Island

Three years ago you stood on this same dock on the South Carolina coast, waiting for the same cabin cruiser to arrive. Across the water you can see the island's lighthouse a few miles away. Memories flood back.

Then, using the name Taylor as you will again, you were on an undercover mission to help the Montagues figure out who was spiriting away valuable jewels and collectibles from their island mansion and replacing them with counterfeits. It took all summer, but eventually you succeeded.

Now your mission is very different. After you received word from Gordon Montague that he had received a mysterious package that included a coded message, you met with him. That was two weeks ago. After you expressed some concern about the package, he accepted your suggestion to be his guest again this summer. But this time, it is he who does not know your real purpose.

The other guests are milling about the dock as the boat approaches. They are much younger and more athletic-looking than the group of three years ago. You recognize Alistair on the deck, who greets the guests as soon as the boat docks. The pilot, no doubt Nolan, remains unseen.

Minutes later, the boat leaves for Montague Island. Less than half an hour later you arrive alongside one of the two docks that flank the marina. Everyone disembarks and follows Alistair up what for you is a very familiar path, forking in three directions after several minutes' walk. The middle path is the one that leads everyone uphill through woods to reveal a large clearing with a three-story mansion surrounded by gardens, greenhouses, and some sheds. A cottage is visible behind and to the right of the mansion.

As the other guests enter the mansion's foyer, it is apparent that they have not been here before, as they begin buzzing about the works of art visible from the foyer: paintings in the art gallery to the left, tapestries and sculptures in the lounge to the right.

"Gordon and Nina Montague will be joining you at dinner in one hour. Meanwhile, our housekeeper Sandy and I will show you to your rooms in the guest wing. There are 15 rooms for the seven of you, but things will get more crowded in a few weeks when the sailing club arrives."

An hour later, the guests are assembled in the dining room when the Montagues enter, dressed in semiformal attire. Gordon and Nina are in their late and mid-50s, respectively. Both are retired, although Gordon remains on a few corporate boards and Nina occasionally does consulting work for her old law firm. Once she began practicing law, she never resumed her earlier acting career.

Gordon speaks first. "Nina and I welcome you to a new season of puzzles, games, and competitive sports on our island. As you know, during your weekends here, each of you will be asked to solve puzzles, play games, and sometimes act out the role of a character in a mystery story in which a crime has been committed. When there is such a mystery, as there will be Sunday, you will become detectives whose goal is to solve the crime. At least one of you will be the person who committed the crime; but even if your character is guilty, you will not know this until you have solved the mystery like the other players.

"Sometimes on the night before a mystery puzzle, an envelope will be slipped under each of your doors, containing specific instructions you will need to follow. The most important thing in your instructions is the key statement or statements that you must provide to other players when they question you. Such statements will always be true when spoken by an innocent character, but may or may not be true when spoken by a guilty party. You may embellish the phrasing of a key statement, provided you are very careful not to change its essence.

"As we have in the past, we ask our guests to call us, as well as each other, only by first names. You will use your own first names in all mystery games, but other facts about you, such as your occupation or your favorite book, may be fictitious facts made up for purposes of a particular story.

Nina continues the orientation. "A prize will be awarded at the end of the summer to the guest who has been the first to correctly solve the most mystery puzzles. When you have a solution to a mystery, you may present it to Gordon, myself, or any of our staff. We will verify that it is correct and complete, and note the time you gave it to us. Of course, this means it is in your interest to get statements from everyone else as quickly as possible—and not just from the other guests. Gordon and I, as well as our six full-time employees, will all participate as characters in most of our mystery stories. When you question Gordon or me or one of our staff, you can rely on our statements to be true. If ever any of the rules Gordon and I have just explained change for a particular mystery, we will let you know.

"You have met Alistair, our head of staff; our other employees who live here are chef Evelyn, gardener Grant, nurse Lyle, secretary Charlotte, and housekeeper Sandy.

"We will be your hosts for 12 of the next 15 weekends including this one, roughly running from Memorial Day to Labor Day. There are three weekends—those three, seven, and eleven weeks from now—when Gordon and I have other commitments, so you have will those off to relax back on the mainland."

Before retiring for the night, Gordon announces, "A little warm-up puzzle will be waiting for you in the lounge after dinner. And tomorrow, you'll get to know one another better when you solve a puzzle we made up based on the information you supplied when you applied to be our guests this season. Have a good night."

Key Deductions

After dinner the guests assemble in the lounge, where 12 metal boxes numbered 1 through 12 sit on a table. A note left by the Montagues explains:

Each of these boxes is locked. They all require different keys to be opened. The keys to boxes 1, 2, and 3 are labeled and are on the table. Boxes 1, 2, and 3 each contain a single key that will open one other box. Six of the other boxes contain a key, but three do not. Two of those that do not contain a key are empty, and the third contains a prize.

Taped to each of the 12 boxes is an index card on which a true statement is printed, as shown. The challenge is to determine which keys are in which boxes and which box contains the prize. Opening each of the boxes 1, 2, and 3, for which you already have keys, will lead to finding sequences of other keys, including the keys to all 12 boxes. Each of the three sequences eventually leads to opening a box that does not contain a key, and the sequence using the most keys ends with the box containing the prize.

So the puzzle is, of boxes 1, 2, and 3, which one should you open to get to the prize?

This box contains the key to box 4 or 10.	This box contains the key to box 5 or 6.	This box contains the key to box 7 or 8.
Box 1	Box 2	Box 3
This box contains the key to box 10 or 12.	This box contains the key to box 11 or no key.	This box contains the key to box 5 or no key.
Box 4	Box 5	Box 6
This box contains the key to box 9 or no key.	This box contains the key to box 10 or no key.	This box contains the key to box 7 or 10.
Box 7	Box 8	Box 9
This box contains the key to box 6 or 11.	This box contains the key to box 8 or 9.	This box contains the key to box 4 or 8.
Box 10	Box 11	Box 12

The New Guests

Saturday morning, Gordon Montague hands each of the guests a puzzle he and Nina have constructed to help the everyone become better acquainted. Apart from you, Taylor, who finished school quite some time ago, all the guests are graduate students or recent graduates from different universities. In this puzzle the universities are identified indirectly, by the name of the school's nickname for its sports teams. Each guest has studied a specific subject matter, and is also an enthusiast of a particular sport.

From the following clues, can you match the guests' first names to their school nickname, field of study, and sport?

1. The guests—Abby, Emma, Greg, James, Logan, Olivia, and Taylor—have or are earning degrees in economics, history, mathematics, music, philosophy, physics, and psychology, not necessarily in that order, at schools with sports nicknames Bears, Bulldogs, Cougars, Lions, Panthers, Tigers, and Wildcats, again not necessarily in that order.

2. Each guest is a sports enthusiast in a different one of the following: curling, golf, lacrosse, rugby, tennis, Ultimate, and volleyball.

3. The areas of study for Abby, Emma, and Greg are philosophy, physics, and psychology, not necessarily in that order.

4. Logan, Olivia, and Taylor are lacrosse, rugby, and volleyball enthusiasts, not necessarily in that order.

5. The students of economics, history, and physics are from schools with the nicknames Bears, Lions, and Wildcats, not necessarily in that order.

6. Golf, Ultimate, and volleyball are the sports of the Bulldog, Cougar, and Wildcat, not necessarily in that order.

7. The golf enthusiast, who is not the Wildcat, will be giving lessons to James and the student of music.

8. The volleyball enthusiast will be giving lessons to three other guests: Olivia, the economics student, and the Wildcat.

9. The Bear's field of study is not history, and the Panther's field is not mathematics or music.

10. The historian is not the lacrosse, rugby, or tennis enthusiast.

11. Neither Abby nor the Bear, who is not Taylor, is the curling or tennis enthusiast.

12. Abby is not the student of psychology, and Taylor is not the student of music.

13. Greg is not the Panther, and the student of mathematics is not the Cougar.

14. The student of economics is not the rugby enthusiast.

15. The physicist's sport is not curling or tennis, and the philosopher's sport is not golf.

Murder in the Game Alcove

The seven regular guests are playing the roles of corporate officers who are using Montague Island as a weekend retreat. An eighth person from the corporation—the bookkeeper, played by housekeeper Sandy—is found dead in the game alcove late in the afternoon.

From the statements of the staff and guests, can you determine each guest's corporate title, which luxury item he or she owns, and who killed the bookkeeper?

Statements by the Montagues:

1. Gordon: The titles of the seven corporate officers are chief executive officer (CEO), president, vice president of marketing, vice president of research, comptroller, secretary, and treasurer. There are rumors that money was being embezzled from the company by one of these officers, with the help of the bookkeeper.

2. Nina: The seven corporate officers are all quite wealthy, as evidenced by some of the luxury items they have purchased in recent years, which include a private airplane, a vintage Aston Martin automobile, the rare inverted Jenny postage stamp, a South Pacific island, a ski chalet, a van Gogh painting, and a yacht, all of which were purchased by different officers. The bookkeeper, by contrast, seemed to be a person of modest means.

Statements by the staff:

3. Alistair: There is only one killer, and the killer does not make a false statement.

4. Charlotte: I saw the victim enter the small game room just after 4:30 P.M.

5. Evelyn: I found the victim's body in the game alcove at 5 P.M. A cushion from the small game room was near the body and must have been used to muffle the sound of a gunshot.

6. Grant: The owners of the island and the yacht, neither of whom is Emma, were not in the mansion at the time of the murder.

7. Lyle: The CEO, the president, and the owner of the van Gogh were in the lounge from before 4:30 P.M. until after 5. Around 4:45, the president had a brief discussion with me there.

Statements by the guests:

8. Abby: The vice president of marketing, comptroller, and secretary own the island, ski chalet, and yacht, in some combination.

9. Emma: Abby, James, and I are the vice president of research, comptroller, and treasurer, in some combination.

10. Greg: I am not the secretary or the owner of an island.

11. James: I am not the owner of the inverted Jenny stamp. I was in the library from 4:30 until 5.

12. Logan: James, Olivia, and Taylor own the airplane, the Aston Martin, and the inverted Jenny, in some combination.

13. Olivia: The Aston Martin is not owned by the vice president of research, nor by anyone who was in the lounge at 4:45.

14. Taylor: I do not own an airplane, and I have never spoken with Lyle. Emma was not in the lounge between 4:30 and 5.

Film Festival

A week ago, the guests were invited to bring three movies with them when they returned to the island this weekend. The movies were to have a whimsical common theme of some kind, such as similarities in their titles rather than in subject matter. And so the guests brought in Blu-ray discs, DVDs, and even a few VHS tapes of sets of three films whose titles: begin with a month (*August Rush, September Dawn, October Sky*); begin with an animal (*Elephant Walk, Horse Feathers, Whale Rider*); begin with a planet (*Jupiter Ascending, Mars Attacks!, Saturn 3*); begin with *Blue* (*Blue Jasmine, Blue Valentine, Blue Velvet*); end with *8* (*BUtterfield 8, Jennifer 8, Super 8*); end with *People* (*Fierce People, Funny People, Ordinary People*); and end with *-ully* (*Bully, Sully, Tully*).

After reading descriptions of the films they weren't familiar with, the guests all voted to choose one film from each set of three to be part of a film festival to be held nightly at the mansion during the week of the regatta. Every guest voted for one film in each of the seven categories, and the film with the most votes in each category became part of the film festival. If two films tied for the most votes within a category, the person who brought them in got to break the tie.

From the clues below, can you determine which guest brought in which set of films, how many votes each film received, and which seven films ended up in the film festival?

1. No film was a unanimous choice, and no two guests' films received the same distribution of vote totals. That is, if one guest's three films' vote totals were 4, 2, and 1, no other guest's films received a combination of 4, 2, and 1 votes.

2. The films that received two votes were brought in by Abby, James, and Taylor.

3. The films that received three votes all began with a month, a planet, or *Blue*.

4. Emma, James, and Logan brought in the movie titles beginning with a month, ending in *8*, and ending in *People*, in some combination.

5. *Blue Valentine* received the same number of votes as *Mars Attacks!*.

6. *Sully*, which was not one of Abby's films, received the same number of votes as *Blue Velvet*. In its category, *Sully* finished ahead of *Bully* but behind *Tully*, which received the same number of votes as *Whale Rider*.

7. *Saturn 3* received more votes than either Emma's or Olivia's second-highest vote getters, but one of Logan's films received fewer votes than any of Olivia's three films.

8. *Fierce People* received more votes than *Funny People*, and these two films' combined vote total was equal to the number of votes received by *Jupiter Ascending*, which received fewer votes than *October Sky*.

9. *August Rush* and *Super 8* received the most votes in their categories, while *BUtterfield 8* came in third.

10. The guest who brought in the two films that shared first place in their category resolved the tie in favor of the film that came first alphabetically.

Logic puzzle grid.

Column headers: 6-1-0, 5-1-1, 5-2-0, 4-2-1, 4-3-0, 3-3-1, 3-2-2, begins with a month, begins with an animal, begins with a planet, begins with *Blue*, ends with *8*, ends with *People*, ends with *-ully*

Row labels: Abby, Emma, Greg, James, Logan, Olivia, Taylor, begins with a month, begins with an animal, begins with a planet, begins with *Blue*, ends with *8*, ends with *People*, ends with *-ully*

votes

Title	votes
August Rush	
September Dawn	
October Sky	
Elephant Walk	
Horse Feathers	
Whale Rider	
Jupiter Ascending	
Mars Attacks!	
Saturn 3	
Blue Jasmine	
Blue Valentine	
Blue Velvet	
BUtterfield 8	
Jennifer 8	
Super 8	
Fierce People	
Funny People	
Ordinary People	
Bully	
Sully	
Tully	

Bookshelf

One shelf in the library is reserved for Gordon Montague's seven favorite game-related books, which are arranged from left to right in alphabetical order: *Bridge Squeezes Complete*; *The Compleat Strategist*; *Encyclopedia of Chess Variants*; *A Gamut of Games*; *Invincible: The Games of Shusaku*; *Rook Endings*; and *Winning Ways for Your Mathematical Plays*. One at a time, each of the seven guests take turns borrowing one or two books from the shelf and putting them back on the shelf before the next guest borrows any books.

The guests are careless about returning the books to the same places on the shelf from which they took them. In fact, after all seven guests were done borrowing and returning books, the order of books on the shelf was the complete reverse of how the books were originally arranged.

From the guests' statements, can you determine the order in which they must have borrowed and returned books?

1. Abby: I borrowed the first book on the left and the last book on the right, and I switched their places when I put them back. The last borrower before me was Logan.

2. Emma: The books I borrowed were fourth and fifth from the left, but I put them back as the sixth and seventh books from the left, respectively.

3. Greg: I borrowed the last book on the right but made it the third book from the left when I put it back.

4. James: I borrowed the second book from the left and the second book from the right, and I switched their places when I put them back.

5. Logan: I borrowed the first book on the left but made it the second book from the left when I put it back.

6. Olivia: I borrowed the second and fifth books from the left and switched their places when I put them back.

7. Taylor: I borrowed the second and third books from the left and switched their places when I put them back.

Six, Zero

The Montagues are kibitzing a logic-oriented word game being played by the guests. It's a variation on the classic deduction game of bulls and cows, or the trademarked games Mastermind and Jotto.

One player—in this case, Taylor—thinks of a secret word, which must be a reasonably common, uncapitalized six-letter word composed of six different letters of the alphabet. The other players take turns guessing the word aloud, and after each guess (which must also be a reasonably common six-letter word composed of all different letters) Taylor states a pair of numbers. The first number indicates the number of letters in the guess that match letters in the secret word and are in the same position within the word, and the second number indicates how many letters in the guess are in the secret word but are not in the same position.

For example, if the secret word were HORNET and the guess were BROKEN, Taylor would say "one, three," since one matching letter (E) is in the same position in both words, and three other letters (N, O, R) are also in both words but in different positions.

The first five guesses and Taylor's replies are:

Abby:	PLAYER	0, 2
Emma:	INTAKE	2, 1
Greg:	SAILOR	0, 4
James:	DETAIL	1, 3
Logan:	SALINE	2, 3

At this point Olivia says, "I know what the secret word is!" Do you?

Synchronized Walking

On Saturday morning the seven guests—Abby, Emma, Greg, James, Logan, Olivia, and Taylor—are joined by Nolan, who is the Montagues' cabin cruiser and helicopter pilot, and his new girlfriend Cheryl, to take walks on various routes around the island. Each of the nine participants starts at one of the following locations: Boathouse, Bridge, Lighthouse, Lookout Point, Mansion, Old Well, Pond, Sea Caves, Windmill. No two start at the same location.

Wearing synchronized watches, all the people begin their walks at the same time. Sixty-five minutes later, each ends up at one of the locations where one of the others started. From the following clues, can you determine each person's starting location, route, and ending location?

1. Within a few seconds, the number of minutes each guest took to travel between each pair of locations (walking along the paths in either direction) was always as follows:

   > Mansion to Bridge: 10
   > Bridge to Pond: 10
   > Pond to Old Well: 10
   > Bridge to Windmill: 30
   > Windmill to Old Well: 25
   > Old Well to Sea Caves: 10
   > Old Well to Lookout Point: 15
   > Lookout Point to Boathouse: 45
   > Boathouse to Mansion: 10
   > Boathouse to Lighthouse: 15

2. No one traveled on any part of his or her route more than once.

3. No two people both ended up where the other one had started. That is, if one person began at location A and ended up at location B, the person who began at B did not end up at A. (However, people who started at locations A and B could both end up at another person's starting location.)

4. James and Taylor reached the bridge 30 minutes into the walk, and one of them continued on toward the location the other had just come from. No one else was at the bridge at the same time.

5. Cheryl, Emma, Taylor, and Olivia passed by the mansion in that order; none of them started or ended at the mansion.

6. Abby, Greg, Logan, and Nolan passed by the windmill in that order; none of them started or ended at the windmill.

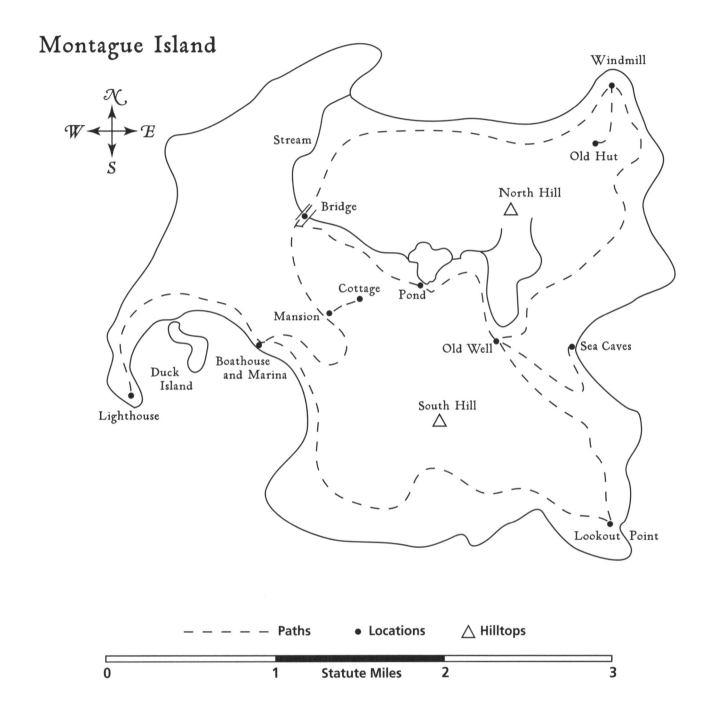

Montague Island

| --- --- --- | Paths | ● Locations | △ Hilltops |

0   1   Statute Miles   2   3

Murder at the Embassy

In this murder mystery concocted by Gordon Montague, the mansion is transformed into an embassy hosting a wine-tasting party for diplomats, held in the lounge and screened porch. During the party, a visiting dignitary—played by nurse Lyle—is found dead in the lounge, the victim of a fast-acting poison. Prior to the party, each guest was given a written instruction specifying the statement he or she is to make when questioned by other guests.

Statements by the Montagues:

1. Gordon: The seven diplomats—played by the guests Abby, Emma, Greg, James, Logan, Olivia, and Taylor—are actually spies for their countries. In no particular order, those countries are Atlantea, Elysia, Halcyonna, Lemuria, Shalomar, Ulteria, and Wyvernia. Our staff members know which spies are from which countries.

2. Nina: Each spy has a code name known to our staff. Those names are Basilisk, Chimaera, Dragon, Griffin, Kylin, Sphinx, and Unicorn.

Statements by the staff:

3. Alistair: Three spies passed on information to three other spies during the party. The seventh spy was there to assassinate the dignitary played by Lyle, and is the only guest whose statement may be a lie. With people moving around and distracting one another with conversation, all the spies had the opportunity to poison the victim's wine glass.

4. Charlotte: The spies from Atlantea, Halcyonna, and Wyvernia have the code names Griffin, Kylin, and Unicorn, not necessarily in that order.

5. Evelyn: For a time prior to the murder, three people were sitting together at a table on the screened porch: Logan, the Kylin, and the spy from Wyvernia. One of them left and a new person joined them, and now the group consisted of Taylor, the Unicorn, and the spy from Lemuria. A few minutes later one of them left, and another person—who was not one who had left the table previously—joined them, and now the group consisted of James, the Sphinx, and the spy from Elysia.

6. Grant: For a time prior to the murder, three people were sitting together at a table in the lounge: Abby, the Unicorn, and the spy from Ulteria. One of them left and a new person joined them, and now the group consisted of Olivia, the Griffin, and the spy from Atlantea. A few minutes later one of them left, and the person who had left the table previously rejoined them, and now the group consisted of Greg, the Dragon, and the spy from Shalomar.

7. Sandy: For a time prior to the murder, three people were sitting together on a sofa in the lounge: Emma, the Unicorn, and the spy from Wyvernia.

Statements by the guests:

8. Abby: I gave information to the spy from Elysia. My code name is not Basilisk.

9. Emma: I received information from the spy from Shalomar.

10. Greg: I received information from the spy from Ulteria.

11. James: I received information from the spy from Lemuria. My code name is not Kylin, and I am not from Wyvernia.

12. Logan: I gave information to the spy from Atlantea.

13. Olivia: I gave information to the spy from Wyvernia.

14. Taylor: I gave information to the spy from Halcyonna.

	Atlantea	Elysia	Halcyonna	Lemuria	Shalomar	Ulteria	Wyvernia	Basilisk	Chimaera	Dragon	Griffin	Kylin	Sphinx	Unicorn
Abby														
Emma														
Greg														
James														
Logan														
Olivia														
Taylor														
Basilisk														
Chimaera														
Dragon														
Griffin														
Kylin														
Sphinx														
Unicorn														

A Day of Civilization

After a few practice games that were left unfinished, the guests undertake the challenge of playing a full seven-player game of Civilization—the original game designed by Francis Tresham and published in the United Kingdom by Hartland Trefoil and in the United States by Avalon Hill in 1981 (not to be confused with the many other games having a similar title).

The board is a map of the Mediterranean Sea and surrounding lands, divided into many irregularly shaped regions. Each player initially places a single token on a region in his or her nation's starting area, and play begins. The tokens represent population that will grow each turn and eventually form cities that allow players to acquire trade good cards. Those cards allow players to purchase Civilization cards such as Agriculture and Literacy, which confer various advantages during play but are also necessary for advancing a nation along the Archaeological Succession Track from Stone Age to Bronze Age to Late Iron Age. The winner, after struggling to overcome various natural and manmade calamities, is the player whose nation first reaches the end of the track, proving itself to be the most highly developed civilization. Other players can be ranked second through seventh based on their track location as well as the value of their Civilization cards, trade good cards, and treasury.

The game lasts 12 hours, which is typical for a seven-player game. From the clues below, which are based on the Montagues' observation of the game, can you determine who played which nation, who was hard-hit by which calamity, and the order in which the players finished?

Note: If a clue states that one player finished "ahead of" or "behind" another player, it does not necessarily mean "just ahead of" or "just behind"; other players may have finished in between.

1. Abby, Emma, Greg, James, Logan, Olivia, and Taylor each chose a different nation to play from the following: Assyria, Babylon, Crete, Egypt, Illyria, Italy, Thrace.

2. During the course of the game, each player's nation was hit particularly hard by a different one of the following calamities: civil war, earthquake, epidemic, famine, flood, piracy, volcanic eruption.

3. Abby, Emma, and Olivia played the nations whose calamities were civil war, famine, and a volcanic eruption, in some combination.

4. The nation that suffered from an epidemic, which was not Italy, finished behind Thrace but ahead of Illyria.

5. Greg finished behind Egypt but ahead of the nation that was ravaged by flood.

6. Italy finished behind the nation that had a civil war but ahead of Abby.

7. James finished behind Crete but ahead of Assyria, which did not finish last.

8. The nation that was hurt by famine finished ahead of Babylon.

9. The nation that was devastated by a volcanic eruption finished ahead of Olivia.

10. Taylor finished ahead of the nation that was hit hard by piracy, which finished ahead of the nation badly damaged by an earthquake.

11. Abby finished better than Greg but worse than Olivia.

12. Illyria finished better than Egypt but worse than Crete.

The Memorable Mosaic

As a memory test, each guest is given three minutes to study a mosaic made up of a rectangular array of 90 square tiles, and then is asked to try to redraw the mosaic. Since the most common tile color in the mosaic is white, a guest only needs to remember where the other tiles were located. Each of those tiles is either gray or black. The positions of the 42 white tiles are shown in the diagram (for instance, row 8 contains one white tile, in column 6). The guests were each given such a diagram to complete by indicating which of the remaining 48 squares contained gray tiles and which contained black.

No guest was able to reconstruct the mosaic perfectly, but some came close. From the following accurate recollections of the guests, can you determine the locations of the gray and black tiles?

The final pattern may appear random but in fact contains a coded message (more about that soon).

1. There are 28 gray tiles and 20 black tiles.

2. Every row contains at least one gray tile, and only one row has no black tile.

3. Row 1 has the same number of black tiles as row 6.

4. Rows 3 and 4 have the same number of gray tiles.

5. The number of black tiles in row 9 is equal to the total number of black tiles in rows 3 and 4.

6. Three rows each have exactly three black tiles.

7. Tiles in rows 7 and 9 match in color within each column except when one of them is white.

8. In no column are the tiles in rows 8 and 9 the same color.

9. The row with five black tiles and two gray tiles is the only row in which there are more black tiles than gray.

10. Every column contains at least one black tile, and column 6 has more black tiles than any other column.

11. Three tiles that are the only black tiles in their columns, one of which is in row 5, share a diagonal.

12. One row contains exactly three adjacent black tiles, and two other rows—neither of which is row 3—each contain one pair of adjacent black tiles. These are the only three places where black tiles are horizontally adjacent.

13. The most gray tiles appearing consecutively in any column is three, occurring only once. The next most is two, occurring five times.

14. No two gray tiles in row 9 are adjacent.

15. Only column 2 contains more than one black tile that is directly below a white tile.

16. There is only one black tile directly above another black tile. Of the two diagonal lines of tiles that include the upper tile of that pair, each includes a black tile that is the only black tile in its column.

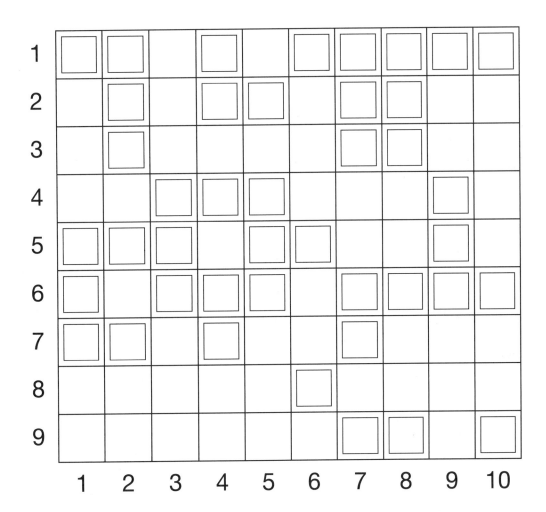

"The people from the sailboat club will be arriving next weekend," Gordon says, as the two of you walk past the pond. "We've been getting the other guest rooms ready."

"Looking forward to it," you reply. "Now about where we're going. The mosaic was the key to understanding the coded message you received. It seems that whoever sent you the first message wanted to get your attention, and then sent you the mosaic to help you understand the message."

"The mosaic came without a note or return address," Gordon recounts, "but it did come with a new copy of the code sent previously."

The original message consisted of nine five-digit numbers arranged in a column (shown at right). You told Gordon that you would try to decipher it, but you reported success only after the mosaic came.

03600
33104
37505
50241
01081
20100
03817
77374
55806

"The mosaic has tiles of three colors," you explain. "That suggested numbers in base 3, in which the only digits are 0, 1, and 2. Just as 10 represents ten in base 10 and two in base 2 (binary), 10 represents three in base 3. The number eight would be written 22 (two threes plus two ones), and the number nine would be written as 100. The original message contained no numbers higher than 8, which means that each digit could be represented by a two-digit number in base 3. If you rewrite the message that way and then replace each 0 with a white tile, each 1 with a gray tile, and each 2 with a black tile, you end up with the precise tile pattern of the mosaic."

You recall the numerical equivalent of the mosaic pattern (shown at right).

"And you have deciphered it?" Gordon asks, as you near the old well.

0010200000
1010010011
1021120012
1200021101
0001002201
0200010000
0010220121
2121102111
1212220020

"There are 26 letters in the alphabet," you continue, "one less than 3×3×3. So every number from 0 through 26 can be represented by a three-digit number in base 3. A very simple substitution cipher is to represent the letter A with a 1, B with a 2, C with a 3, and so on, up to Z = 26. If instead you replace these numbers with their three-digit base 3 equivalents, you get A = 001, B = 002, C = 010, up to Z = 222 (two nines plus two threes plus two ones). The fact that there are nine lines in the message, and in the mosaic, suggests reading down the columns in groups of three digits, and then translating those three-digit numbers to letters according to this substitution code. And when you do, this message reveals itself: DIG TEN PACES WEST OF OLD WELL. A series of three white tiles was used to represent spaces between words."

"So that's why you're carrying a shovel," Gordon says. "Well, we're almost there."

Using your cellphone's compass app, you walk about ten yards due west of the edge of the well. A patch of dirt looks as though it may have been dug up recently. After a few minutes of digging, you hit a metal box, which you hand to Gordon to open.

"Are you sure this is safe?" he asks.

"No one intending you harm would have gone to all this trouble," you reply confidently. "I'm sure it's something else entirely."

Gordon opens the box and finds a photo of a university building. "That's the college I attended," Gordon murmurs.

There is also a handwritten note, which simply says: RECALL STRANGE GAMER ART. Gordon has no idea what any of it means.

Three-Card Poker

The seven guests—Abby, Emma, Greg, James, Logan, Olivia, and Taylor—are joined by Nolan and Cheryl for a few hands of three-card poker. The game is similar to regular poker, but there are only three cards in a hand. Unlike in five-card poker, straights outrank flushes (see box below).

Under the house rules the players agreed upon, after being dealt three cards, each player has the option of discarding one or two of them, drawing replacements from the deck. In the first hand, all nine players chose to discard two cards. The nine single cards they held, before drawing new cards from the deck, were, in no particular order, ♡A, ♡Q, ♡J, ◇K, ◇Q, ◇J, ♣A, ♣J, and ♣10.

Cheryl wondered aloud about which set of three players could make the best three-card poker hand from the single cards they had kept, and asked all the players to write down their cards so she could find out at the end of the hand. Later, she made a puzzle in which the object was to determine from the following clues which single card each player held after discarding.

1. Abby and Nolan held cards of the same rank.

2. Logan and Olivia held cards of the same rank.

3. Olivia's card was higher than Emma's.

4. Logan's card was not the same suit as Cheryl's or James's.

5. The cards held by Emma, Greg, and Nolan made a better hand than those held by Greg, James, and Taylor, which in turn made a better hand than the cards held by Emma, Nolan, and Olivia, which in turn made a better hand than the cards held by Abby, Emma, and Greg, which in turn made a better hand than the cards held by Abby, Logan, and Taylor.

What card did each player hold?

Ranks of Three-Card Poker Hands (Highest to Lowest)

straight flush: three cards of the same suit in sequence, such as ♠Q ♠J ♠10; aces can be high or low

three of a kind: three cards of the same rank

straight: three cards in sequence, not all of the same suit, such as ◇9 ♣8 ♡7

flush: three cards of the same suit, not also forming a sequence

pair: one pair of cards of the same rank

nothing: none of the above

In the case of two straights or straight flushes, the higher one wins. If two hands contain pairs, the one with the higher pair wins, regardless of the other card. But if two hands contain the same pair, the hand with the higher third card wins. In the case of two flushes or two hands with nothing, the hand with the highest card wins. If the hands have the same highest card, the second-highest cards are compared, and if necessary the third-highest cards. Ties can occur.

Murder in the Morning

The Montagues have prepared an unusual assortment of puzzle activities for the seven regular guests as well as Nolan, who is staying in the cottage this weekend. Besides participating in the activities, Nolan will also play the role of the victim in a planned murder mystery.

Four rooms in the mansion—the art gallery, small game room, sitting room, and screened porch—have been set up with a number of puzzle and game activities. The morning is divided into ten 20-minute periods, of which the first begins at 8:30 A.M. and the last ends at 11:50 A.M. Participants planned in advance which rooms they would visit during which periods, and the Montagues reviewed and approved the schedules.

As the 10th and final 20-minute period ends, only seven of the eight participants are accounted for: Nolan is missing. His body is later discovered hidden somewhere in or near the mansion. (It's just an act, of course.) From the set of clues below, which were compiled from the schedules submitted by the participants, and the statements of the staff and guests, can you identify the killer or killers?

Clues:

1. Each person (Abby, Emma, Greg, James, Logan, Nolan, Olivia, and Taylor) visited each of the four activity rooms exactly once—the art gallery, small game room, sitting room, and screened porch, not necessarily in that order. Each person spent one 20-minute period in one room, two 20-minute periods in another room, three 20-minute periods in another room, and four 20-minute periods in another room, not necessarily in that order.

2. Two participants were present in each of the four rooms in both the first and 10th periods—or would have been, had the victim managed to complete his schedule.

3. Only Abby, Emma, and Logan spent more time in the small game room than in the screened porch, and only James, Logan, and Taylor spent more time in the art gallery than in the sitting room.

4. The art gallery and screened porch tied for the most visits lasting four periods, and the sitting room alone had the next most four-period visits.

5. Emma, Greg, Logan, and Olivia each spent three periods in the small game room; no one else did the same.

Number of periods staying at each location

	art gallery				screened porch				sitting room				small game room			
	1	2	3	4	1	2	3	4	1	2	3	4	1	2	3	4
Abby																
Emma																
Greg																
James																
Logan																
Nolan																
Olivia																
Taylor																

6. Logan and Taylor started the morning's activities in the sitting room and finished in the small game room, while Abby and Greg started in the small game room and finished in the sitting room.

7. The most participants together in the same room for any single period was four, when Abby, Greg, James, and Logan were all in the art gallery during period 4.

8. Emma, Nolan, and Olivia were all scheduled to be in the sitting room in periods 5 and 6.

9. James was alone in the small game room during periods 5 and 6.

10. Emma and Nolan were together during the first period.

11. Two participants changed rooms after period 2, three changed rooms after period 3, and four participants changed rooms after period 4. Nolan was scheduled to change rooms between periods 8 and 9 but had gone missing by then.

Statements by the Montagues:

12. Gordon: The motive for the murder was revenge for the death of a close relative several months ago.

13. Nina: All the participants followed their scheduled movements, except that Nolan only followed it until he was killed. The clues based on these schedules are all to be trusted, as well as any other statements except those given by the killers, who may lie.

Statements by the staff:

14. Alistair: The wounds make it clear that there were two killers who used different stabbing weapons.

15. Charlotte: During the middle of an activity period, there would have been time to commit murder and hide the body somewhere nearby so that the puzzle activities could continue.

16. Evelyn: If Emma is guilty, Logan is not.

17. Grant: The amount of time it took participants to change rooms between periods was negligible, and the murder could not have taken place between periods without someone noticing.

18. Lyle: From the art gallery, small game room, or sitting room, a body could have quickly been hidden in the art studio, game alcove, or sitting room closet.

19. Sandy: From the screened porch, a body could have quickly been moved to the nearby tool shed.

Statements by the guests:

20. Abby: I last saw Nolan during period 7, and he was fine.

21. Emma: Nolan and I were supposed to be in the same room during period 10, but he never showed up.

22. Greg: I never saw Nolan.

23. James: I last saw Nolan during period 7, and he was fine.

24. Logan: I never saw Nolan.

25. Olivia: I last saw Nolan during period 6, and he was fine.

26. Taylor: Nolan and I were supposed to be in the same room during period 9, but he never showed up.

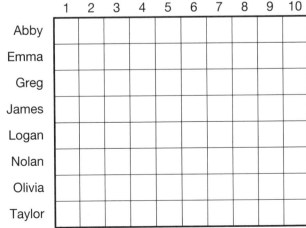

Rooms (AG, SP, SR, or SG) visited, by period

	1	2	3	4	5	6	7	8	9	10
Abby										
Emma										
Greg										
James										
Logan										
Nolan										
Olivia										
Taylor										

Full House

The seven regular summer guests and seven sailing club members have each been assigned one of the 15 guest rooms in the mansion, as shown in the guest wing floor plan, leaving one room empty. From the following clues, can you determine who has been assigned to which room?

1. The regular guests (Abby, Emma, Greg, James, Logan, Olivia, and Taylor) and sailing club members (Brent, Derek, Maria, Phoebe, Rory, Siobhan, and Zach) were all assigned to different rooms.

2. On one floor, three regular guests occupy all three rooms on one side of the hall.

3. Zach is directly below, directly above, and directly across the hall from other sailing club members.

4. Derek is directly below, directly above, and directly across the hall from regular guests.

5. Olivia and Taylor are directly across the hall from one another.

6. The same number of sailing club members occupy A rooms and E rooms.

7. Logan and James are either in adjacent rooms on the same side of the hall, or directly across the hall from one another.

	1A	1B	1C	1D	1E	2A	2B	2C	2D	2E	3A	3B	3C	3D	3E
Abby															
Emma															
Greg															
James															
Logan															
Olivia															
Taylor															
Brent															
Derek															
Maria															
Phoebe															
Rory															
Siobhan															
Zach															

regular summer guests / sailing club members

8. Greg is two floors directly below Rory.

9. Phoebe is two floors directly below Siobhan.

10. Emma is two floors directly below Logan.

11. Maria and Taylor have rooms with the same letter.

Guest Wing

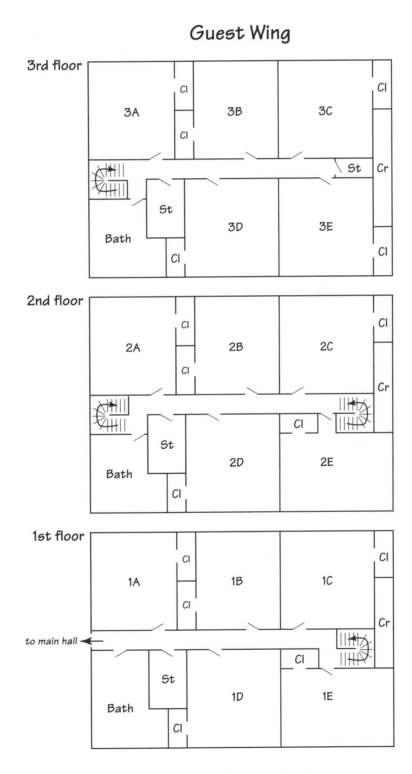

Cl = Closet   St = Storage   Cr = Crawlspace

Sailing the Seven Seas

The seven sailing club members have brought their boats to Montague Island for part of the summer, where a series of races is planned for the week after next. The sailboats are all Club 420 dinghies, which are ideal for racing with two-person crews. (The 420 in the name indicates the length of the boats in centimeters.)

On Saturday, the seven club members—Brett, Derek, Maria, Phoebe, Rory, Siobhan, and Zach—give sailing lessons to the regular guests—Abby, Emma, Greg, James, Logan, Olivia, and Taylor. On Sunday, each club member is randomly paired with one of the regular guests to form a two-person crew for a race around the island. The sailboats' names are *Sea Anemone, Sea Horse, Sea Lion, Sea Otter, Sea Robin, Sea Star,* and *Sea Urchin.*

From the following clues, can you determine how the seven club members and seven guests were paired up, which boat each pair was in, and the order in which everyone finished?

1. Emma, Logan, and Olivia were paired with Derek, Siobhan, and Zach, not necessarily in that order.

2. The sailboats used by Maria, Rory, and Zach were the *Sea Horse,* the *Sea Otter,* and the *Sea Robin,* not necessarily in that order.

3. Greg, James, and Taylor were on the *Sea Anemone, Sea Otter,* and *Sea Robin,* not necessarily in that order.

4. Logan's boat finished ahead of the *Sea Lion,* which finished ahead of Derek's boat.

5. Brent's boat finished three places better than the *Sea Anemone.*

6. The *Sea Horse* finished three places better than Abby's boat.

7. Emma finished two places better than Siobhan, who in turn finished two places better than the *Sea Urchin.*

8. Rory finished ahead of the *Sea Otter.*

9. Taylor finished ahead of Maria.

10. Greg and Olivia finished one place apart.

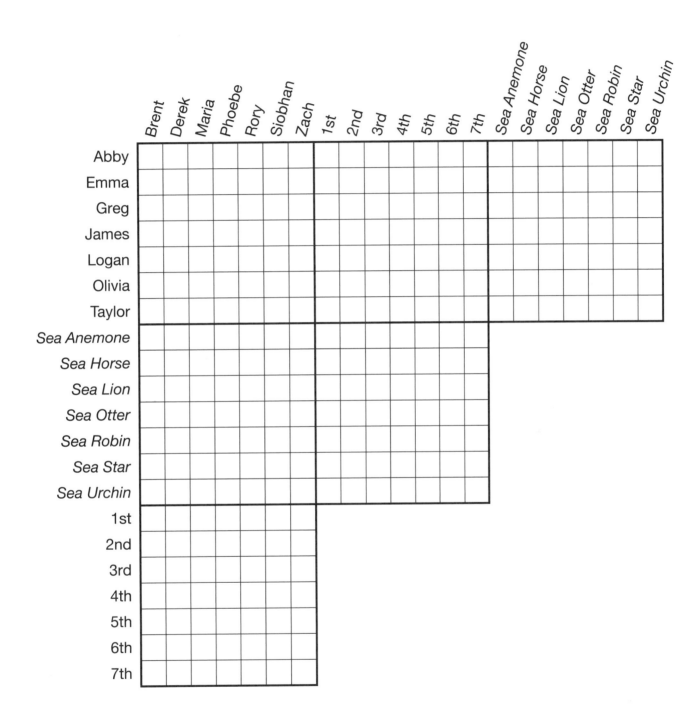

Secret Passages

Gordon Montague hands out a floorplan of the mansion to his guests and explains: "A unique feature of Montague mansion is its extensive network of secret passages. In 1973, when the mansion was about a century old, it was bought by a man named Terence Plumly, who made extensive updates and renovations, including the addition of crawlspaces that can be used to move around the house secretly. In fact, everywhere that a crawlspace borders a closet or storage area on this floorplan, there is a removable panel between the closet or storage area and the crawlspace. In addition, Plumly added tunnels leading from basement 2 to two crawlspaces that contain ladders leading up to any of the three floors in the guest wing and either of the two floors in the staff wing. A third crawlspace, in the front of the house, is accessible from basement 1 via its storage area; it divides into two and leads up to the spaces behind the foyer closets as well as (through closets) the small game room bathroom and sitting room on the second floor, and the master bedroom on the third floor.

"I have prepared a puzzle that you will need to solve collaboratively. I have placed seven beautifully crafted burr puzzles, which have interlocking wooden pieces that can be tricky to take apart and put back together, in the following seven rooms: the art studio, the dining room, the private study, guest room 2D, and staff rooms S3, S5, and S7. I have randomly assigned you the following starting positions: Abby, guest room 2E; Emma, guest room 3C; Greg, guest room 3D; James, special guest room SG1; Logan, special guest room SG2; Olivia, the sitting room; and Taylor, the small game room. For your reference, I've written your names in the appropriate rooms on the floorplan and circled them, and shaded in the rooms where the burr puzzles are located.

"Your challenge is to plan seven routes that will take each of you to a different burr puzzle without any two of you ever visiting the same room, basement, or crawlspace, and without anyone crossing anyone else's path. Paths may, however, go above or below one another if they are on different floors. You may not backtrack or go outside the house. Two of you may both visit the same hallway, but only if you are never in the same part of that hallway. The secret passages may all be used, and the doors connecting the tunnels to basement 2 are unlocked, as are all of the doors in the house.

"Note that the guest wing does not connect to the other wings on the second or third floors. For purposes of this puzzle, the landing that can be reached from two different first-floor hallways and two different second-floor hallways, as well as from the foyer, is not considered to be part of the foyer. Basements 1 and 2 are considered to be separate rooms.

"If you are successful, you all get to keep the burr puzzles as prizes. For a successful solution, it is sufficient to tell me which of you will end up in which of the burr puzzle rooms. Good luck."

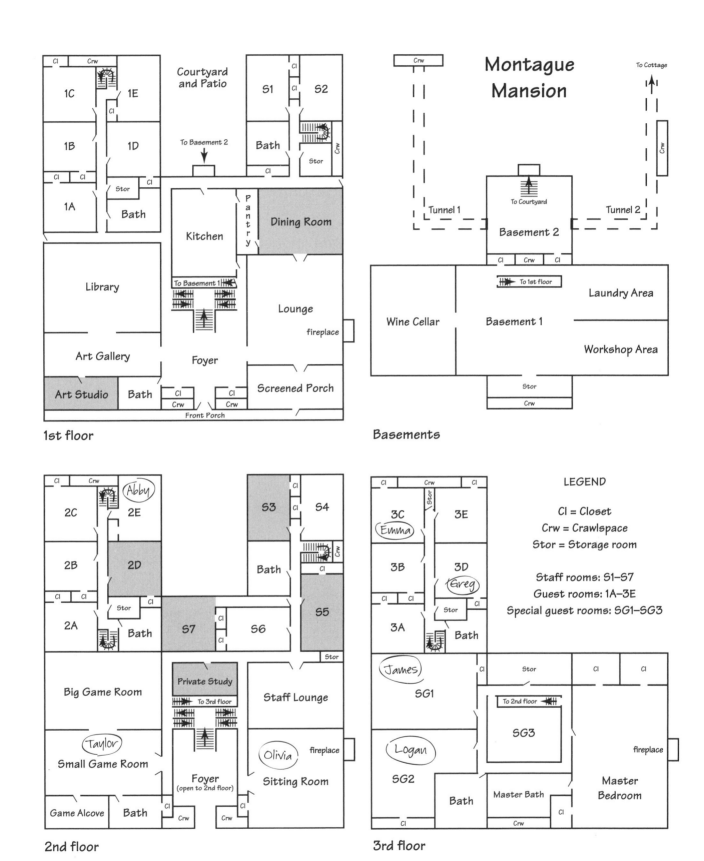

1st floor

Cl · Crw
1C · 1E
Cl
1B · 1D
Cl · Cl · Cl
1A · Stor
Bath

Courtyard and Patio
To Basement 2

S1 · Cl · S2
Cl
Bath
Stor
Crw
Cl

Kitchen · Pantry · Dining Room
To Basement 1
Library · Lounge
fireplace
Art Gallery · Foyer
Art Studio · Bath · Cl · Screened Porch
Crw · Cl · Crw
Front Porch

Basements

Crw

Montague Mansion

To Cottage
Crw

Tunnel 1 · To Courtyard · Tunnel 2
Basement 2
Cl · Crw · Cl
To 1st floor · Laundry Area
Wine Cellar · Basement 1
Workshop Area
Stor
Crw

2nd floor

Cl · Crw · Cl
2C · (Abby) 2E · S3 · Cl · S4
2B · 2D · Bath · Crw · Cl
Cl · Cl · Stor · Cl · S5
2A · Bath · S7 · Cl · S6 · Cl · Stor
Big Game Room · Private Study · Staff Lounge
To 3rd floor
(Taylor) Small Game Room · Foyer (open to 2nd floor) · (Olivia) Sitting Room · fireplace
Game Alcove · Bath · Cl · Crw · Cl · Crw

3rd floor

Cl · Crw · Cl
3C (Emma) · Stor · 3E
3B · 3D (Greg)
Cl · Cl · Stor · Cl
3A · Bath
(James) SG1 · Cl · Stor · Cl · Cl
To 2nd floor
(Logan) SG3 · fireplace
SG2 · Bath · Master Bath · Cl · Master Bedroom
Cl · Crw

LEGEND

Cl = Closet
Crw = Crawlspace
Stor = Storage room

Staff rooms: S1–S7
Guest rooms: 1A–3E
Special guest rooms: SG1–SG3

Name Games

The Montagues have asked each guest to compose a quiz for the other guests to take. Their written instructions are as follows:

"Each quiz will consist of seven clues, each of which should point to the name of a different guest (the guest's first name only, as per our usual custom). These quizzes are the basis for a dual competition in solving and quiz writing. Each of you will be given copies of the quizzes that the other guests make, and you will be allotted 30 minutes to solve as many of the quizzes as you can. (No one will take their own quiz, of course.) You will earn 1 point for each correct answer in each quiz. You will also earn 2 points for each guest who fails to solve any questions in the quiz you created, provided that at least one guest correctly answers at least one question on your quiz. If no one solves any question on your quiz, you will get no points for quiz writing—so you may want to make your quiz hard, but not impossible. The guest with the most total points from solving and quiz writing wins the event.

"Although there is no penalty for an incorrect guess, you may want to consider whether a lucky guess on a hard quiz might earn quiz-writing points for someone whose quiz no one else may be able to solve. Good luck."

After receiving everyone's quiz and answer key, the Montagues make enough copies for everyone and pass them out. The quizzes are shown on page 36.

From the clues below, can you determine who wrote each quiz, what each guest scored on each quiz, and everyone's total points? (As a bonus, you may wish to see how you would have done on the quizzes.)

1. Emma, Greg, and Logan wrote quizzes 3, 4, and 6, in come combination.

2. The number of guests scoring 0 was different for each quiz, except that quizzes 1 and 3 each had one score of 0. A guest does not score 0 for the quiz he or she wrote, but simply receives no score for that quiz.

3. Once a guest figured out the principle behind a quiz, he or she usually solved it entirely and earned a score of 7, and altogether the guests recorded 21 scores of 7. Otherwise, as happened at least 16 times, the score was usually 0.

4. Four guests—none of whom were Emma or Logan—were in the middle of solving quizzes 2, 3, and 7 when time ran out, and earned scores of 2, 3, 4, and 6 on one of those quizzes. (Guests did not solve the quizzes in numerical order, but jumped around to find ones that they could solve most easily.)

5. Abby earned a 5 on quiz 5 by virtue of making an educated guess that turned out to be only partially correct. Had she simply skipped that quiz, she would have won the event instead of finishing second.

6. Olivia's score on quiz 3 was exactly half James's score on that same quiz.

7. The number of 0's Greg scored on quizzes was equal to the number of guests who scored 0 on quiz 6, one of whom was Greg.

8. Greg earned 1 solving point less than Logan.

9. Despite earning a 7 on quiz 7, James finished with fewer solving points than Olivia.

10. More guests scored 0 on James's quiz than on Olivia's.

11. James, Logan, and Olivia all scored the same on quiz 6 as they did on quiz 5.

12. All eight scores earned by Abby and Taylor on quizzes 1, 2, 3, and 4 were the same.

13. Greg scored 0 on quizzes 3 and 7.

14. Guests taking quiz 2 scored more 0's than guests taking quiz 4, but fewer 0's than guests taking quiz 7.

	scores earned							writer of							solving points	quiz-writing points	total score
	Quiz 1	Quiz 2	Quiz 3	Quiz 4	Quiz 5	Quiz 6	Quiz 7	Quiz 1	Quiz 2	Quiz 3	Quiz 4	Quiz 5	Quiz 6	Quiz 7			
Abby																	
Emma																	
Greg																	
James																	
Logan																	
Olivia																	
Taylor																	
scores of 7																	
scores of 0																	
other scores																	

Name Games (continued)

Here are the seven quizzes composed by the guests. The instructions for each quiz are the same: Answer each clue with one of the seven guests' names (Abby, Emma, Greg, James, Logan, Olivia, Taylor). No guest's name will be the answer to more than one question on the same quiz.

Quiz 1

1. I dreamt of being on a pirate ship sailing to Tripoli via the Suez Canal.
2. I enter the research lab by using an electronic key in the elevator.
3. If you stay, lordship, you may be subject to arrest by the Crown.
4. I'm very sorry if I seem mad at times, because normally I'm not.
5. I prefer jelly to jam, escarole to other endives, and pears to peaches.
6. My blog and website are devoted to the history of puzzles.
7. One big regret of mine is not having studied Japanese in college.

Quiz 2

1. 51
2. 77
3. 125
4. 151
5. 1019
6. 1214
7. 2018

Quiz 3

1. AIL, HEAD, ASTER, QUALITY, NAIL
2. INK, PAL, RIPE, RID, EVER
3. LOPE, OVER, ARCH, CORN
4. PAST, BAR, HER, GRIM
5. RANGE, AMP, CON, END, RATE, STERN
6. RUN, TUB, SCAR, PEAR, TANG, SEA
7. THIN, CAPE, MAN, RAN

Quiz 4

1. GZBOLI
2. LORERZ
3. OLTZM
4. QZNVH
5. TIVT
6. VNNZ
7. ZYYB

Quiz 5

1. 005227
2. 075621
3. 147334
4. 315204333
5. 331472063
6. 571430301
7. 716123863

Quiz 6

1. BIDS, JUMPY, QUIZ, THIEF, VEX, WRECK
2. BOXY, CONK, FLAT, HOLD, JUMP, QUIZ, VOWS
3. BOXY, CONK, FLIGHT, PROD, QUIZ, VOW
4. BUZZ, FED, HEX, JUMP, QUERY, STUNG, WRECK
5. COPY, FLIGHT, JURY, KIND, OUTBOX, QUIZ, VOWS
6. CROWS, FLIGHT, MINK, OUTJUMP, QUIZ, VEXED
7. CUB, FED, JUMP, QUIZ, VEXING, WHISK

Quiz 7

1. All jokes a magician ever says are a form of misdirection.
2. Get ready, everyone, get set, count to three, and go.
3. Here are the photos taken at yesterday's lavish office reunion.
4. Mostly vegetarians live in this land of grapes and nuts.
5. My favorite team caught a bad break yesterday.
6. Our logo is very important as a way to identify our products.
7. Some people watch every monster movie and TV show.

Snark Hunting

Nina Montague has gathered the guests in the library for a reading of Lewis Carroll's poem *The Hunting of the Snark*. Afterward, she presents the guests with a puzzle that she says was inspired by the poem.

"On this table are 10 envelopes numbered from 1 through 10. Inside each envelope are two cards, each showing one of the letters S, N, A, R, K. Some of the cards are blue and some are green. Which five envelopes should you choose in order to have enough letters to spell SNARK with both all green cards and all blue cards?

"There are two combinations that work, but rather than trying to guess which envelopes to choose, first determine which letters are in each envelope, and what colors their cards are, from the following clues."

1. Each envelope contains one blue card showing one of the letters S, N, A, R, K, and one green card showing a different one of those same five letters.

2. In the 10 envelopes combined, each of the five different letters appears on two green cards and two blue cards.

3. No two envelopes contain the same combination of two letters.

4. No two envelopes with consecutive numbers contain the same letter.

5. Neither envelope 1 nor 2 contains a K.

6. Neither envelope 7 nor 8 contains an A.

7. Envelope 6 does not contain both an A and a K.

8. The sum of the numbers of the envelopes that contain a green card with an A equals the sum of the two lowest-numbered envelopes that contain a K, both of which K's are on blue cards.

9. The sum of the numbers of the envelopes that contain an R is 7 more than the sum of the numbers of the envelopes that contain an N.

10. An N on a green card is in the highest-numbered envelope of the four that contain N's.

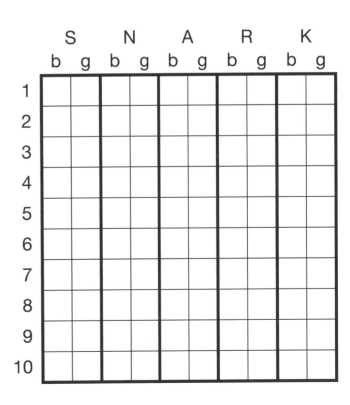

37

Regatta

A series of seven sailboat races took place over the past seven days, beginning on a Sunday and ending on a Saturday. Each of the seven guests was paired with a different one of the seven sailboat club members each time. Each member of the two-person crew earned 1 point for finishing first, 2 points for finishing second, and so on, up to 7 points for finishing seventh (last). At the end of the seven races, point totals were calculated for each guest and each sailing club member. The guest and sailing club member with the lowest point totals were awarded trophies.

In the first race, guests and club members were paired in mutual alphabetical order, after which a logical rotation took place. Here are the pairings for all seven races:

Race 1	Race 2	Race 3	Race 4	Race 5	Race 6	Race 7
Abby–Brent	Abby–Derek	Abby–Maria	Abby–Phoebe	Abby–Rory	Abby–Siobhan	Abby–Zach
Emma–Derek	Emma–Maria	Emma–Phoebe	Emma–Rory	Emma–Siobhan	Emma–Zach	Emma–Brent
Greg–Maria	Greg–Phoebe	Greg–Rory	Greg–Siobhan	Greg–Zach	Greg–Brent	Greg–Derek
James–Phoebe	James–Rory	James–Siobhan	James–Zach	James–Brent	James–Derek	James–Maria
Logan–Rory	Logan–Siobhan	Logan–Zach	Logan–Brent	Logan–Derek	Logan–Maria	Logan–Phoebe
Olivia–Siobhan	Olivia–Zach	Olivia–Brent	Olivia–Derek	Olivia–Maria	Olivia–Phoebe	Olivia–Rory
Taylor–Zach	Taylor–Brent	Taylor–Derek	Taylor–Maria	Taylor–Phoebe	Taylor–Rory	Taylor–Siobhan

From the following clues, can you determine the order in which each pair finished each race and the final point totals for all 14 participants?

1. One sailing club member finished in last place in four races in a row, and another finished last twice in a row. Phoebe finished last only once.

2. Emma, Greg, and James never finished last in any race.

3. In race 4, Taylor finished one place better than Olivia, who finished one place better than Logan.

4. One sailing club member finished first in races 4, 5, and 6.

5. Logan never finished first.

6. James finished first twice.

7. In the first six races, Siobhan finished in every possible position from first through sixth once each.

8. In race 7, Olivia finished one place better than James, who finished two places better than Greg.

9. One sailing club member finished the last three races in third, second, and first place, in that order.

10. In both races that Taylor won, Olivia finished fifth and Greg sixth.

11. James did better than Abby in races 4 and 6.

12. Maria finished sixth twice.

13. A guest who ended up with 19 total points finished third three times in a row.

14. Taylor finished three places better than Emma in race 7.

15. Olivia and Greg finished second in races 2 and 3, respectively, their best results, and the only time either of them ever finished in that position.

16. Two guests were tied for the fewest points among guests after six races.

17. The winning club member had 3 fewer points than the second-place finisher. The sum of their final point totals was equal to the point total of another club member.

	Race 1	Race 2	Race 3	Race 4	Race 5	Race 6	Race 7	total points
Abby								
Emma								
Greg								
James								
Logan								
Olivia								
Taylor								
Brent								
Derek								
Maria								
Phoebe								
Rory								
Siobhan								
Zach								

regular summer guests

sailing club members

Murder in the Wine Cellar

In this murder mystery scripted by the Montagues, the mansion is hosting a meeting of the Coastal Stamp and Coin Collectors club, of which the seven guests are playing members. Grant, the Montagues' gardener, is playing another club member. At 6 P.M., chef Evelyn goes to the wine cellar and finds that Grant has been murdered.

From the statements of the Montagues, the staff, and the guests, can you determine who attended which meetings of the club and identify the killer?

Statements by the Montagues:

1. Gordon: The eight club members—played by the guests Abby, Emma, Greg, James, Logan, Olivia, and Taylor, and our gardener Grant—have been meeting during the past year at various locations along the East Coast. This weekend at Montague Island is their eighth club meeting. Grant attended three of the first seven meetings, and each of the other members attended exactly four of the first seven.

2. Nina: The killer acted alone and is the only person who may give a false statement. However, the killer will not give a false statement about which club meetings anyone attended, since several others would be all too likely to make statements that contradict the killer's.

Statements by the staff:

3. Alistair: Sometime during one of the first seven club gatherings, Grant secretly witnessed one of the club members stealing rare coins from a display case. Grant began blackmailing the thief, who killed him instead of meeting Grant's latest payment demand.

4. Charlotte: The first seven meetings of the club took place in Atlantic City, Fort Lauderdale, Montauk, Myrtle Beach, Newport, Savannah, and Williamsburg, although not in that order. The coin theft incident took place during a weekend meeting that was later than the second meeting but prior to the sixth meeting.

5. Evelyn: The last time I saw Grant was at 5 P.M., when he was in the staff lounge. I found him dead when I went down to the wine cellar at 6 P.M. He had been hit over the head with a bottle of champagne.

6. Lyle: Two guests who both attended the sixth club meeting were in the big game room between 5 and 6 P.M.

7. Sandy: Emma was in the lounge between 5 and 5:30 P.M., then walked directly to the library. The Montauk meeting, as well as the third and sixth meetings, were each attended by five members. The other meetings were attended by four members each, prior to all eight members attending the Montague Island meeting.

Statements by the guests:

8. Abby: From 5 to 5:30, I was in my room. From 5:30 to 6, I was in the library with Emma. Two of the club meetings I attended were in Atlantic City and Savannah, not necessarily in that order, and the other two meetings at which I was present were the fifth and seventh meetings.

9. Emma: Between 5 and 5:30 P.M., I was in the lounge. From 5:30 to 6, I was in the library with Abby. I did not attend the club meeting in Myrtle Beach.

10. Greg: Between 5 and 6 P.M., I was on the second floor. I saw Grant at three of the four club meetings I attended: Savannah, Montauk, and Newport.

11. James: Between 5 and 6 P.M., I was in my room. I attended the Fort Lauderdale club meeting as well as the following one. The other two meetings I attended were the sixth and seventh meetings. The second and seventh meetings were the only two attended by both Abby and me.

12. Logan: Between 5 and 6 P.M., I was in my room. I attended the Williamsburg meeting, as did Abby, Greg, and Olivia.

13. Olivia: Between 5 and 6 P.M., I was in my room. Emma and I were both at the first, third, and fourth club meetings. I did not attend the Myrtle Beach meeting.

14. Taylor: Between 5 and 6 P.M., I was playing pool in the big game room. I attended consecutive club meetings in Atlantic City and Montauk, not necessarily in that order. Emma and I were both at the third, fourth, and sixth meetings.

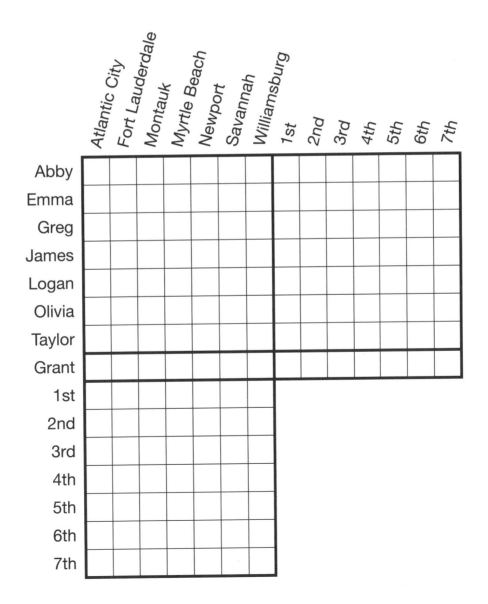

41

Speed Darts

Nolan has suggested that he and the seven guests have a very short darts competition in the large game room. Instead of playing a traditional darts game such as 301 or 501, players have agreed that each will simply throws three darts and score their totals. After each player has thrown three darts, the four players with the highest totals will move to a second round. Scores do not carry over to the next round, and again each player will throw three darts. The two highest scorers will continue on to a third round, in which whoever scores the higher total wins the competition.

Scoring is standard. A dart scores the number that appears outside the wedge-shaped area it lands in, except that it scores double if it lands in the narrow outer ring or triple if it lands in the smaller ring that runs through the middle of each wedge. A dart in the bullseye area scores 25 in the outer bullseye and 50 in the inner bullseye.

Given the clues below, can you determine what numbers each player's darts scored each round and who won the event?

1. Each dart scored at least 1 point, but remarkably, no two of the 42 darts thrown in the competition scored the same.

2. Even more remarkably, each set of three darts that each player threw in a given round formed a straight line that, if extended, also ran through the center of the target. That is, if a player's darts included no bullseyes, that player's darts were either all in a single wedge-shaped area or in two areas directly opposite one another on the dartboard (such as 20 and 3 or 1 and 19); any bullseye, outer or inner, can be part of any such straight line.

3. The eight players' three-dart totals were 28, 60, 61, 63, 66, 73, 75, and 78 in the first round. The totals in the second round were 82, 87, 89, and 92, and in the third round they were 94 and 100.

4. In the first round, players Olivia and Taylor each hit the single, double, and triple values of a single number.

5. In the first round, all six darts thrown by Abby and Emma lay along the same line (as described in clue 2).

6. All the shots thrown by James in the first round and by Taylor in the second round lay along the same line.

7. All the shots thrown by Greg in the first round and by Nolan in the second round lay along the same line.

8. All the shots thrown by Logan in the first round and by Olivia in the second round, which included one 25-point outer bullseye by Olivia, lay along the same line.

9. All the shots thrown by Nolan in the first round and by Taylor in the third round, which included one 50-point inner bullseye by Taylor, lay along the same line.

10. The first-round shots of Olivia and Taylor, the second-round shots of Abby, and the third-round shots of Nolan were thrown in four different lines, none of which was ever used by anyone else.

11. One of Logan's darts scored 2 points.

12. In terms of the second-highest scoring single darts thrown in the first round, the players ranked as follows, from highest to lowest: Olivia, Taylor, Emma, Greg, Nolan, Abby, James, Logan.

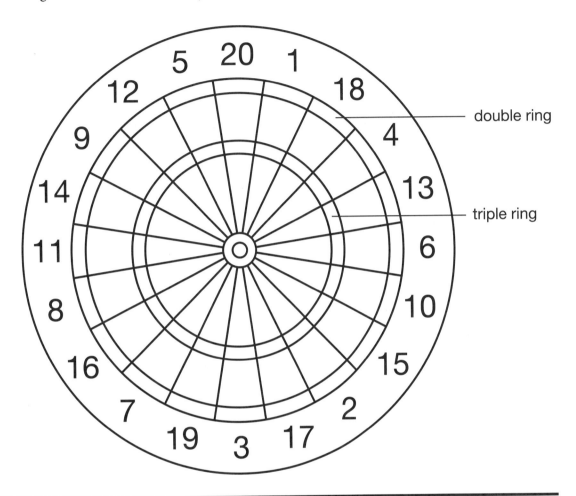

"Are you sure you want to continue with this?" you ask the visitor who is looking over your shoulder as you write down a series of numbers.

"Yes, I want to see it all the way through. Here's the next thing to hide, preferably in a safe indoor location."

Your visitor hands you a small wooden box containing a small, decorated ceramic pot. You recognize it as pre-Columbian, possibly from Peru.

"All right, then. I know a place in the greenhouse where it won't be noticed or disturbed. But I would like to reserve the right to tell him something—not everything, just enough so he's not worried after he finds this." Your visitor nods approval.

You continue encoding a message, just as you did before, and think about how long to wait before mailing it.

Web of Lies

Another murder has been committed on Montague Island, if only in the imaginations of Gordon and Nina Montague. The guests and staff act out the script as usual, except that no one portrays the victim. A complete solution requires only the name(s) of the guilty party or parties.

Statements by the Montagues:

1. Gordon: I had arranged for a philatelist from the mainland to bring some rare postage stamps for me to inspect and possibly purchase. Nolan brought him to the island on the cabin cruiser, but returned to the mainland to run another errand, taking Lyle and Sandy along. I sent Alistair to meet the boat and lead the visitor to the mansion, but when they hadn't shown up by noon as expected, Grant and I took the path toward the marina and found Alistair dazed and the visitor dead. His stamps had been stolen.

2. Nina: At the time of the murder, I was upstairs in the sitting room. Between 11:30 A.M. and noon, the guests were in various locations both in and out of the mansion.

Statements by the staff:

3. Alistair: The stamp dealer and I began walking from the marina toward the mansion when I was hit over the head from behind by something hard. I was unconscious for several minutes until just before Gordon and Grant arrived. Footprints around the victim's body suggest a struggle with as many as three other people, and the cause of death was likely being struck with one or more blunt objects such as a rock.

4. Charlotte: Only guilty guests' statements may be false, and anyone who makes a false statement is guilty.

5. Evelyn: The four guests who were in the mansion between 11:30 A.M. and noon could not have committed the murder.

6. Grant: The killer or killers may have been hiding in or behind the boathouse when we started walking from the marina to the mansion.

Statements by the guests:

7. Abby: Taylor was in the library from 11:45 until 12:30 P.M.

8. Emma: Taylor was not in the small game room from 11 A.M. until 11:45.

9. Greg: Taylor was in the small game room from 11 A.M. until 11:45.

10. James: Taylor was not in the library from 11:45 until 12:30 P.M.

11. Logan: Regarding Abby and Greg, exactly one of them is lying.

12. Olivia: Regarding Emma or James, they are either both telling the truth or both lying.

13. Taylor: I was in the small game room from 11 A.M. until 11:45 and in the library from 11:45 until 12:30 P.M.

ESP Test

The Montagues have prepared a surprise quiz for the seven guests to take, and the results will form the basis for a puzzle.

Gordon Montague explains:

"In the 1930s, Zener decks were developed for use in testing people for extrasensory perception. Each card shows one of the following symbols: circle, plus sign, square, star, or wavy lines, as you can see here.

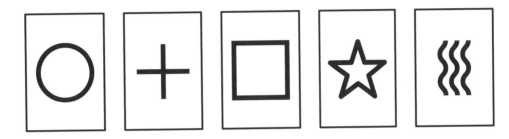

"I took one card with each symbol, shuffled them, and dealt them face-down into a row on this table, so even I don't know the order in which they appear.

"On a piece of paper, please write down your best guess as to the card appearing in each of the five positions, which we'll call 1 through 5 from left to right. Afterward, we'll see how you all did."

Abby, Olivia, and Taylor seem disinterested and quickly write down their guesses. Abby guesses wavy lines for all five cards, Olivia guesses five stars, and Taylor guesses five squares. Clearly they will each get exactly one correct.

The other four guests, however, seem intrigued, and try to concentrate on each card before writing down a guess. Their guesses for how the cards are arranged from left to right are as follows:

> Emma: plus sign, circle, square, star, wavy lines
> Greg: wavy lines, square, circle, plus sign, star
> James: square, plus sign, wavy lines, circle, star
> Logan: wavy lines, circle, circle, circle, star

Gordon looks at the guesses, then looks at the cards without showing them to the guests.

"Emma and James each have two correct guesses," he announces, "and the rest of you each have one. From this information, can you figure out the actual order of the cards?"

Shell Game

Nina Montague has a seashell collection that she has made the basis for the following puzzle, which the seven guests are challenged to solve cooperatively.

On the dining room table are five placemats, on each of which is a set of five matching shells. Placemat 1 has five clam shells, placemat 2 has five conch shells, placemat 3 has five cowrie shells, placemat 4 has five oyster shells, and placemat 5 has five scallop shells. Each guest is to exchange some of the shells on one placemat with some of the shells on one other placemat. The goal, after each of the seven guests has made an exchange of shells between a pair of placemats, is for each of the five placemats to end up with one shell of every type.

Not just any exchanges may be made, however. Nina has printed out a list of allowable exchanges, not necessarily in the order in which they need to be made to solve the puzzle, and offered a hint: Each allowable shell exchange will be used once.

In what order, and between which placemats, should the exchanges be made?

Allowable Shell Exchanges

two clams for three oysters

one clam and one conch for one cowrie, one oyster, and one scallop

one clam and one oyster for two scallops

two conchs for two oysters

three conchs for two cowries

one conch and one cowrie for one clam, one oyster, and one scallop

one conch and one cowrie for two scallops

Truth Counts

After breakfast, Gordon Montague hands out a sheet of paper to each guest. "I have three short exercises in logic for you, which our new friend Cheryl was good enough to suggest. See if you can answer all three correctly."

The questions are as follows. In each case, the word "statement" refers only to a statement given in the puzzle, not some other statement made by the speaker at another time.

1. Three of the guests make the following statements:

Abby: "Either Emma's or Greg's statement is false, but not both."
Emma: "Either Greg's or Abby's statement is false, but not both."
Greg: "Either Abby's or Emma's statement is false, but not both."

Of these three statements, what is the greatest number that can all be true?

2. Four of the guests make the following statements:

James: "Either Logan's or Olivia's statement is false, but not both."
Logan: "Both Olivia's and Taylor's statements are true."
Olivia: "Either Taylor's or James's statement is false, but not both."
Taylor: "Both James's and Logan's statements are true."

Of these four statements, what is the greatest number that can all be true?

3. Seven guests make the following statements:

Abby: "Either Emma's or Greg's statement is false, but not both."
Emma: "Either Greg's or James's statement is false, but not both."
Greg: "Either James's or Logan's statement is false, but not both."
James: "Either Logan's or Olivia's statement is false, but not both."
Logan: "Either Olivia's or Taylor's statement is false, but not both."
Olivia: "Either Taylor's or Abby's statement is false, but not both."
Taylor: "Either Abby's or Emma's statement is false, but not both."

Of these seven statements, what is the greatest number that can all be true?

Beach Volleyball

The seven regular guests are joined by Cheryl and Nolan as well as three members of the sailing club—Rory, Siobhan, and Zach—to form six two-player teams for a beach volleyball tournament. The players pair themselves into teams as follows: Abby and James, Cheryl and Nolan, Emma and Logan, Greg and Olivia, Rory and Taylor, Siobhan and Zach.

Each team wears a pair of bathing suits that match in color, and each team's color is a different one of the following: red, gold, green, blue, white, black.

In order for the tournament to be completed more quickly, play took place on two different courts set up on a sandy area near the marina.

The tournament rules were as follows.

1. The six teams will first play a double round-robin—that is, every team plays every other team twice.

2. The teams that finish with the four best records will advance to the semifinals. If two or more teams tie with the same won-lost record, then: (1) if one team won both its games against the other, it finishes higher; (2) if the teams split their head-to-head games with one win apiece, then their records are compared against the highest-finishing other team, and the one who did better against that highest-finishing other team wins the tiebreak. If there is still a tie, their records against the second-highest-finishing other team are compared, and so on. If they both have the same records against every other team, they will play a tiebreak game (this was not necessary). If more than one set of teams tie in the standings, ties between the teams with the best records are resolved first.

3. In the semifinals, the first-place team plays the fourth-place team and the second- and third-place teams meet. The winners of those games meet in a final championship game.

From the following clues, can you determine each team's record during the double round-robin, the winners of the semifinal games, and the winner of the finals?

1. The team that won just one game was the only team to lose more than half its games in the double round-robin.

2. In the double round-robin, two pairs of teams tied in the standings: the blue and gold teams tied, and the teams of Abby-James and Emma-Logan tied. Gold edged out blue on tiebreak because the gold team had the better record against the black team. The Abby-James team won on tiebreak because of its better record against the team of Rory and Taylor.

3. Of the 15 matches in the double round-robin, nine ended in 1–1 ties. Two of the matches that ended 2–0 were a victory by the team that finished first in the round-robin against the team that finished third in the round-robin, and a victory by that third-place team against the fifth-place finisher in the round-robin.

4. In the semifinal and final games, there was a total of one upset, defined as a win by a team that finished lower in the double round-robin standings than the team it defeated.

5. The white team finished one place better than the red team, which finished one place better than Greg and Olivia.

6. The team of Abby and James finished either two places better or two places worse than the team of Cheryl and Nolan.

7. The final game was between two teams who were 1–1 against one another in the double round-robin.

8. The losing team in the finals was not Siobhan and Zach.

	vs.1	vs.2	vs.3	vs.4	vs.5	vs.6	W–L
1st	X						
2nd		X					
3rd			X				
4th				X			
5th					X		
6th						X	

team won-lost records

	red	gold	green	blue	white	black	1st	2nd	3rd	4th	5th	6th
Abby & James												
Cheryl & Nolan												
Emma & Logan												
Greg & Olivia												
Rory and Taylor												
Siobhan & Zach												
1st						
2nd						
3rd						
4th						
5th						
6th						

Barbecue

After the long day of beach volleyball, everyone was looking forward to a hearty meal, and the Montagues did not disappoint. Putting their two propane grills to full use on the patio, the hosts and staff prepared a variety of foods for the group.

Each of the 12 volleyball players (Abby, Cheryl, Emma, Greg, James, Logan, Nolan, Olivia, Rory, Siobhan, Taylor, and Zach) chose one beverage (fruit punch, iced tea, lemonade, or sarsaparilla), one main course item (chicken, hamburger, ribs, salmon, or veggie burger), one starchy food (baked potato or corn on the cob), one green vegetable (asparagus or zucchini), tossed salad with one kind of dressing (balsamic vinaigrette, blue cheese, French, or ranch), and one flavor of ice cream for dessert (chocolate chip, peach, or pistachio).

From the following clues, can you determine who ate and drank what?

1. Abby, Cheryl, and Greg ordered a hamburger, ribs, and a veggie burger, in some combination.

2. James, Logan, and Nolan ate chicken, ribs, and a veggie burger, in some combination.

3. The three who had salmon were Rory, Siobhan, and the only person to choose blue cheese dressing.

4. Olivia and Taylor both had the same main course as well as pistachio ice cream.

5. Three of the four who had hamburgers used ranch dressing on their salads, and the other one used French.

6. The fruit punch drinkers were Nolan, Siobhan, and the only person to have both a baked potato and balsamic vinaigrette dressing.

7. The three who drank iced tea were Cheryl, Logan, and one of the two people who had both ranch dressing and pistachio ice cream.

8. The three who had peach ice cream, one of whom was James, all had the same beverage but had three different main courses and used three different salad dressings.

9. The three who drank sarsaparilla, none of whom had veggie burgers, include Greg and Zach, who both had chocolate chip ice cream.

10. The four who had zucchini were Greg, Logan, and two people who both used French dressing.

11. More people used balsamic vinaigrette than ranch dressing.

12. Abby, Cheryl, and Emma used balsamic vinaigrette, French, and ranch dressings, in some combination.

13. All the veggie burger eaters had chocolate chip ice cream.

14. Greg and Logan used the same kind of dressing.

15. The three who chose baked potatoes had three different types of ice cream, none of them had a hamburger, and only one of them had asparagus.

16. One of the three people who had pistachio ice cream also had chicken and used French dressing.

17. No one who ate salmon used balsamic vinaigrette.

18. James made the same choice between baked potato and corn as Emma did.

19. Taylor had the same kind of drink as someone who used French dressing.

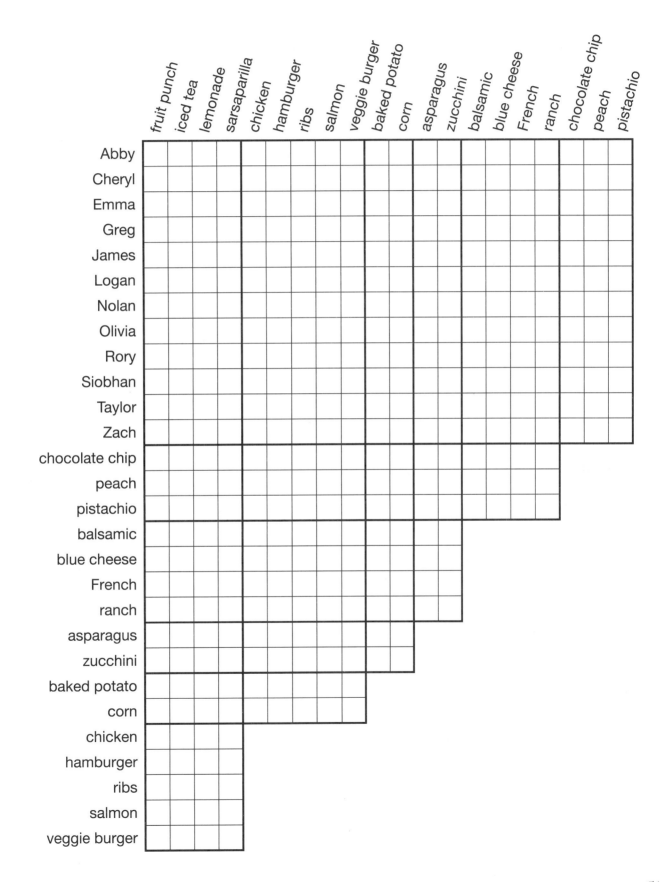

Hide and Seek

The Montagues have invited the guests to take part in a game of virtual hide and seek. There are seven snow globes in the mansion. The premise of the puzzle is that each guest steals one of these snow globes and hides it somewhere on the island. However, to save time and energy, none of the globes will actually leave the mansion, and no one has to go searching for them on foot. Instead, solving the puzzle will tell everyone the whereabouts of the "missing" snow globes, if everyone did what the clues indicate.

From the following clues, can you determine which snow globe was (hypothetically) taken by whom, from which room it was taken, and where each one was hidden?

1. Three snow globes were in the sitting room, and two each were in the library and lounge. Each snow globe contains a miniature replica of a different iconic image: the Alamo, Gateway Arch, Golden Gate Bridge, Mount Rushmore, Space Needle, Statue of Liberty, and Washington Monument.

2. Each snow globe was stolen by a different guest. The seven globes were hidden in seven different locations: the boathouse, cottage, greenhouse, lighthouse, old hut, tool shed, and windmill.

3. James, Logan, and Olivia hid snow globes in the lighthouse, old hut, and windmill, in some combination.

4. Snow globes depicting the Gateway Arch, Golden Gate Bridge, and Washington Monument were hidden in the cottage, greenhouse, and lighthouse, in some combination.

5. Greg, James, and Taylor took the snow globes depicting the Gateway Arch, Space Needle, and Washington Monument, in some combination

6. Neither James, nor the guest who hid a snow globe in the lighthouse, nor the person who took the Washington Monument snow globe, removed a snow globe from the library.

7. The snow globes from the sitting room did not end up in the cottage, old hut, or windmill.

8. The Alamo snow globe, which did not end up in the windmill, and the snow globe taken by Abby came from the same room.

9. The Space Needle snow globe and the one taken by Greg came from the same room.

10. One of the two snow globes in the library was taken by Olivia, and the other one, which was not taken by Emma, ended up in the tool shed.

11. The Statue of Liberty and Gateway Arch snow globes were in the same room.

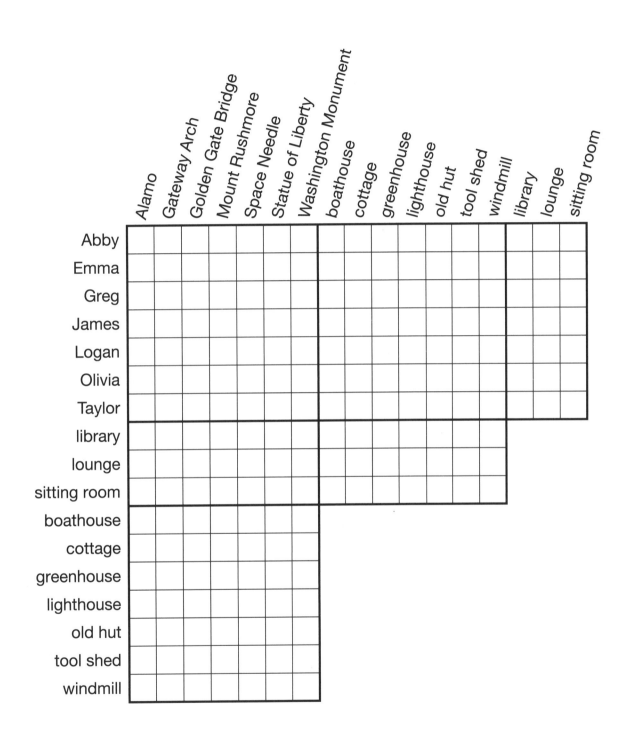

To the Lighthouse

Match all the guests other than Taylor to the occupations they are assuming in this mystery, determine the order in which Taylor spoke to the other guests, and identify the killer.

Statements by the Montagues:

1. Gordon: All seven guests—Abby, Emma, Greg, James, Logan, Olivia, and Taylor—were in the dining room until 1 P.M., and all seven met in the lounge at 2 P.M. Only one guest is guilty, and it is not Taylor. All guests are truthful about the statements Taylor made to them.

2. Nina: The guests other than Taylor are playing the roles of architect, beachcomber, cartographer, diplomat, engineer, and farmer. Abby, Emma, and Olivia are the architect, engineer, and farmer, in some combination. The three true statements made by Taylor, along with all the other statements by Gordon, myself, and the staff, are sufficient to determine a unique guilty party.

Statements by the staff:

3. Alistair: Shortly after 2 P.M., I discovered that a visitor from the mainland who had left the mansion around 1 P.M. to walk to the lighthouse had been stabbed to death on the path between the boathouse and the lighthouse. It would have taken a guest more than half an hour to make a round trip from the mansion to the scene of the crime and back.

4. Charlotte: Olivia was in the mansion between 1 and 2 P.M., but was not in the big game room. If neither Abby nor Emma is guilty, then Emma is not the farmer.

5. Evelyn: Taylor spoke to James just before speaking to Emma, and to Greg just before speaking to Abby.

6. Grant: The third guest Taylor spoke to was neither the cartographer nor the diplomat, and the last guest Taylor spoke to was the beachcomber.

7. Lyle: Taylor spoke to Abby sometime before speaking to Emma.

8. Sandy: Between 1 and 2 P.M., one guest was in the big game room, the beachcomber and the farmer were in their respective guest rooms, and the architect and the cartographer were in the library.

Statements by the guests:

9. Abby: Taylor told me that Greg was not in the library between 1 and 2 P.M.

10. Emma: Taylor told me that Olivia is not the farmer.

11. James: Taylor told me that the engineer was not in the big game room between 1 and 2 P.M.

12. Logan: Taylor told me that Greg was in the library between 1 and 2 P.M.

13. Greg: Taylor told me that Olivia is the farmer.

14. Olivia: Taylor told me that the engineer was in the big game room between 1 and 2 P.M.

15. Taylor: I was in the dining room between 1 and 2 P.M. After that, I listened to the guests' various accounts of their whereabouts during that hour, after which I met with each guest privately and made a statement. The statements I made to three of the guests were true, but my statements to the other three guests were false. I never made two true statements in a row or two false statements in a row.

	architect	beachcomber	cartographer	diplomat	engineer	farmer	guest room	library	big game room	outdoors	1st	2nd	3rd	4th	5th	6th
Abby																
Emma																
Greg																
James																
Logan																
Olivia																
1st																
2nd																
3rd																
4th																
5th																
6th																
guest room																
library																
big game room																
outdoors																

Shooting Match

Gordon and Nina Montague have assembled the regular guests, along with Nolan, Cheryl, and two cottage visitors who are friends of Nolan and Cheryl, Vince and Isabel. Gordon explains the afternoon activity they have planned for the group.

"Inspired by the popularity of the survival scenario of *The Hunger Games* books and films and the online video game *Fortnite*, Nina and I have developed a nonviolent game in which players 'shoot' other players by taking photos of them with their phones' cameras, which you all have. Simply put, Player X earns a point for taking a picture of Player Y before Player Y takes a picture of Player X. Once X has 'shot' Y, Y can no longer earn a point for shooting X, although all the other players are still fair game for both X and Y to shoot—no one gets eliminated in this game.

"In a few minutes, at 12:45 P.M., all of you will leave the mansion and go wherever you wish. No photos taken before 1 P.M. will count, and remember that photos on your phones will all bear time stamps that I will review. From 1 P.M. until 3 P.M., your goal is to take photos of as many other players as you can before they take yours. Whoever takes the most valid photos by 3 P.M. will be rewarded with a prize from our art collection. To count, photos need to be of sufficient quality to clearly identify the subject. You may photograph more than one player in a single shot and get credit for shooting each player in the picture. In case of ties, the player who has been photographed fewer times will win, and further ties will be broken in favor of the player whose final photo was taken earlier."

Nina continues: "You may go anywhere you wish on the island. Of course, this being meant as a fair game, no one is allowed to steal or interfere with anyone else's phone, nor disguise themselves so as to be unrecognizable. The only other rule is that the mansion is off limits during the game. If two people shoot each other's pictures almost at once, so that both photos bear the same time stamp, we'll rely on your honesty to tell us who shot first. Good luck."

As the players get ready to depart, several of them become engaged in a heated conversation. Some shake their heads and walk away, while others come closer and appear interested in what's being discussed.

A little after 3 P.M., the 11 players return to the mansion one at a time, handing their phones to the Montagues for scoring. Afterward, each player makes an accurate statement about what happened during the game, and the Montagues also make a comment. From these statements, can you determine who won the game and how each player scored?

Abby: Shortly after 1 P.M. I took a photo of Greg and Vince at the boathouse. Over an hour later, I got separate photos of the only person to end up having taken just one photo and the only person who ended up having been photographed only by me. I was disappointed to learn that I didn't win the game.

Cheryl: While leaving the mansion, I declined an invitation to join a five-player alliance proposed by Vince, as I thought I detected a flaw in the plan that I might be able to exploit. Sure enough, I was able to get a shot of three of the five together by going through the woods toward South Hill and sneaking up on the boathouse from the southeast. Then, without ever being shot, I took a trip through the woods to the path between the old well and the pond, where I encountered another player around 2:00, after which I circled around the pond to the bridge, where I met someone else during the final quarter hour of the game. These were the last two encounters I had during the game, and in each of them one of us shot the other.

Emma: I first went to the bridge, walked up the path to the pond and hid there just off the path. When someone emerged from the woods nearby around 1:30, I took his picture before he could take mine. But in my other four encounters, I was the one whose picture was taken.

Greg: I took a picture of Vince and Isabel early in the game. Later on, I did successfully shoot Emma, and no one shot me doing it, but those were the only two photos I managed to take.

Isabel: I went along with Vince's alliance idea and let myself be shot by two players in return for shooting a photo of two other players. I got a photo of another player later on, but was photographed at the same time by James.

James: I started by cutting through the woods near the cottage to the path near the pond, where someone surprised me and took my picture. I decided to head toward the old well, but I encountered one other player there around 2:00. After that I wandered south into the woods, where I later got a picture of two players, one of whom—who was not Logan—was in the process of photographing the other.

Logan: Someone took a photo of me, Isabel, and Vince at the boathouse, soon after Vince and Isabel took two pictures of me, in each of which I was seen with another player. Later on, just as I was taking Emma's picture, someone took a picture of both me and Emma. No one ever got another photo of me.

Nolan: I started by hiding west of the path between the mansion and the bridge. Soon I snapped a picture of Taylor crossing that path, heading toward me. Much later I got a photo of two other players, one of whom was shooting the other.

Olivia: After hearing the alliance's plans, I headed for the path to the lighthouse and waited near Duck Island for a chance to sneak up on the boathouse from the northwest. Just as the allies were finishing their fifth and final photo, someone came from the other direction and took a shot of three of them, who all took off chasing that person into the woods. But I managed to get a shot of the two who remained. My next encounter was unsuccessful, as I was photographed a short time later, not far from the boathouse. Much later, I encountered Cheryl near the bridge.

Taylor: I initially hid in a greenhouse next to the mansion. When I didn't hear anyone else for a time, I decided to scout around a bit and went west and crossed the path that leads to the boathouse, but I was immediately photographed by someone who was lurking in the woods. A little later, not far away, I was able to take individual photos of both Abby and Olivia. Later, somewhere east of the mansion, someone photographed another player and me as that other player took my picture. Later on, I got a photo of Vince. I never went up to the path that connects the bridge, pond, and old well.

Vince: As planned, my alliance idea got me a photo of two players, including Isabel, but I never got any more, while two allies plus two other players shot me. Each of the five allies took a photo of two other players at the boathouse. I never went up to the path that connects the bridge, pond, and old well.

Gordon and Nina: For the record, valid photos were taken of 31 players. Nine photos showed more than one player, all of whom counted for the picture takers, and 12 showed just one player. No one took a photo of someone who had shot them by the end of the game, nor did anyone take more than one photo of the same player. Tiebreak rules were not needed to determine the winner.

photos taken of

photos taken by	Abby	Cheryl	Emma	Greg	Isabel	James	Logan	Nolan	Olivia	Taylor	Vince	totals
Abby	X											
Cheryl		X										
Emma			X									
Greg				X								
Isabel					X							
James						X						
Logan							X					
Nolan								X				
Olivia									X			
Taylor										X		
Vince											X	
totals												

Double Dates

The Montagues have made up a challenging new elimination game for two players. A bowl contains 366 small folded pieces of paper, each of which shows a different date of the year printed in the format "One January, Two January," etc., up through "Thirty-One December." Players draw one slip of paper at random and secretly look at its date and month.

One player is chosen at random to begin. That player chooses one of the letters on his or her slip of paper and reveals the total number of times that letter appears on the slip, without revealing how many of that letter are in the date and how many are in the month. The opponent must then reveal how many of that same letter are on his or her slip of paper. The opponent then chooses a different letter and reveals how many of it are on his or her slip (the number must be at least one), and the first player does the same for that letter. Players continue to take turns choosing a letter that both players must reveal their count of. The player who makes the play that narrows down the opponent's month and date to a single possibility wins, even if the letter revealed also narrows down the player's own date and month to a single possibility.

Emma and James agree to play. Each draws a slip of paper and looks at it. A coin toss determines that James will go first.

James begins by revealing that he has one B on his slip. Emma replies that she also has one B. Next, Emma reveals that her slip has three E's. James replies that his has four E's.

James then reveals that he has two O's, and Emma replies that she also has two O's. Emma reveals that she has two R's, and James says that he also has two R's.

James calculates that his responses have narrowed down his slip to two possibilities, one of which Emma will have no trouble eliminating on her next turn. After some thought, he reveals a letter that will narrow down Emma's possible slips to a single possibility no matter what answer she gives. He reveals how many of that letter he has, and she reveals a higher number of the same letter.

What letter did James reveal, and what were the dates and months on both of their slips of paper?

"This message came the same way the first one did," Gordon explains. "Sent from a mainland post office without a return address. I used the method you showed me to decode it, which led me to this box. It was hidden behind some planters on a shelf in the greenhouse."

Gordon had brought the box into the private study on the second floor of the mansion and placed it on the desk. You lift up the box and pretend to examine it carefully from all angles, then remove its lid.

"Someone has sent you a gift, it appears," you tell Gordon.

Gordon removes the ceramic pot from the box. "No messages inside. Unless this is a forgery, and a rather good one at that, it could be moderately valuable. But who would send it to me, and why?"

"It looks pre-Columbian to me," you offer, "though I'm no expert. Can you identify where and when it may have been made?"

"I think so. And impossible as it is for me to believe, I see a possible connection between this, the photo of my college, and the note that came with that photo."

Gordon pauses for a moment before continuing. "I never told you this, but I was briefly married when I was only a freshman in college. Eloped, in fact, to get around her parents' objections. We were probably both too young to have made that decision, and it ended badly when her parents insisted on taking her back to their original country in South America. They were wealthy and influential, and she found it too hard to go against their wishes. They had the marriage annulled.

"I've been thinking about that photo and note a lot, and STRANGE GAMER ART could be part of a cryptic crossword puzzle clue suggesting an anagram, or 'strange' version of GAMER ART. And the name of the young woman I married during college was MARGARET. But this can't be from her—she died in an automobile accident less than three years after she returned to South America, as I discovered when I finally had enough resources to try to find her again. There's no question about her death, although her parents were very uncooperative when I tried to learn anything more about her life down there. The interesting thing about this pot, though, is that it could very well be from the very country where her parents lived—or still may live, for all I know, though they would be in their 80s."

You look at Gordon's bewilderment and decide that it's time for an admission.

"Gordon, I have to tell you something. I know who is behind the messages, and why they were sent to you. I am not at liberty to tell you more than that right now, but I can promise that there is no reason at all for you to be worried, and that by the end of the last puzzle weekend of the season all will be revealed to you. I hope you will allow you me to continue on as your guest until then. You see, you were never my client this summer. The person responsible for the messages was, and still is."

Skeletons

The seven guests are acting the parts of seven prominent attorneys with specialties in different areas of the law. One of the seven plans to murder one of the others in order to prevent that person from revealing a skeleton in his or her closet—a dark secret involving professional misconduct that could ruin the would-be killer's reputation and get him or her disbarred. Solving the mystery requires naming both the potential killer and victim.

Statements by the Montagues:

1. Gordon: The seven guests—Abby, Emma, Greg, James, Logan, Olivia, and Taylor—are playing attorneys who specialize in seven different fields of law: corporate law, criminal law, estate law, labor law, litigation, patent law, and tax law, in some combination. None of the guests give false statements, not even the one potential future killer.

2. Nina: The four attorneys who know the dark secrets of others met with me individually to ask my legal advice about whether to report what they know to the bar association. I advised them to do so, and three of the four said they probably would. They did not reveal to me whose secrets they know.

Statements by the staff:

3. Alistair: Emma, the estate lawyer, the litigation lawyer, and the tax attorney have dark secrets that could ruin their reputations and lead to disbarment. One of these secrets is known to two people and two are known to one person each.

4. Charlotte: Those who know the secrets are Abby, Logan, the corporate lawyer, and the patent lawyer.

5. Evelyn: The labor lawyer is not a possible future victim despite knowing a dark secret, because the person whose secret he or she knows is sure the labor lawyer would never reveal it.

6. Grant: Having overheard a conversation between the future victim and Nina, the future killer knows which other lawyer knows his or her dark secret.

7. Lyle: Greg, Logan, and Taylor are the estate, labor, and tax lawyers, in some combination.

8. Sandy: No one knows the litigation lawyer's dark secret.

Statements by the guests:

9. Abby: I know Emma's dark secret.

10. Emma: I would never kill Abby.

11. Greg: I would never kill Olivia.

12. James: I know a dark secret, but it isn't Greg's.

13. Logan: I know Emma's dark secret.

14. Olivia: I know a dark secret, but it isn't the estate lawyer's.

15. Taylor: I have a dark secret, which the patent lawyer does not know about.

	corporate	criminal	estate	labor	litigation	patent	tax	has dark secret	knows dark secret	whose secret known	would-be killer	would-be victim
Abby												
Emma												
Greg												
James												
Logan												
Olivia												
Taylor												
has dark secret												
knows dark secret												
whose secret known												
would-be killer												
would-be victim												

Just Desserts

The seven guests, along with three of their friends from the sailing club, decide to thank the Montagues and their staff for their hospitality by preparing a table of 10 different desserts. Abby, Emma, Greg, James, Logan, Olivia, Rory, Siobhan, Taylor, and Zach each make one of the following, not necessarily in this order: apple pie, brownies, cheesecake, cherries jubilee, chocolate lava cake, coconut flan, crêpes suzette, strawberry shortcake, tapioca pudding, and vanilla soufflé. Later on, each guest eats one dessert. From the clues below, can you determine who made which dessert and who ate which dessert?

1. Each of the 10 dessert makers ate a different dessert.

2. No dessert maker ate his or her own dessert.

3. Abby, Greg, Logan, Rory, and Taylor made apple pie, brownies, coconut flan, crêpes suzette, and vanilla soufflé, in some combination.

4. Emma, James, Olivia, Siobhan, and Zach ate cheesecake, cherries jubilee, chocolate lava cake, strawberry shortcake, and tapioca pudding, in some combination.

5. Abby ate the dessert made by the person who ate the dessert made by the person who ate the dessert made by Greg.

6. James made the dessert eaten by the person who made the dessert that was eaten by the person who made the dessert that was eaten by Zach.

7. Logan ate the dessert made by Taylor.

8. Olivia made the dessert eaten by Emma.

9. The maker of tapioca pudding, who was not James, ate cheesecake.

10. The maker of brownies, who was not Greg, ate crêpes suzette.

11. The maker of the cheesecake ate cherries jubilee.

12. The maker of the coconut flan ate brownies.

13. The maker of crêpes suzette ate vanilla soufflé.

14. The maker of cherries jubilee ate strawberry shortcake.

15. Greg neither made nor ate coconut flan, and did not eat vanilla soufflé.

16. James neither made nor ate cherries jubilee, and did not eat chocolate lava cake.

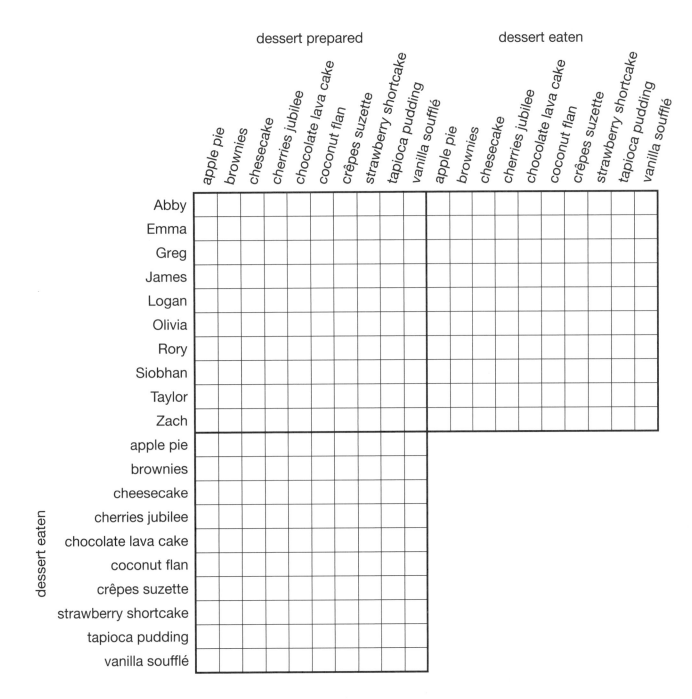

Numbers Game

The Montagues are developing a card game that uses cards that each display a different number. In this version that the guests are testing, the deck consists of 21 cards numbered from 1 through 21.

Each guest is dealt three cards at random, after which guests make verbal offers to exchange one of their cards for one of any other player's cards, saying, for example, "What will someone give me for my 12?" or "Will anyone trade me their 5?" No one is required to exchange cards. After an agreed time limit or after an agreed number of exchanges have been made, players reveal their hands, which are then ranked according to the following rules:

1. All hands consisting of "gap straights" outrank all hands without them. A gap straight is a sequence of three cards in which the gap between the lowest and middle cards, which must be at least 2, is equal to the gap between the middle and highest cards. For example, 1-3-5 is a gap straight with gaps of 2, and 4-9-14 is a gap straight with gaps of 5.

2. Between two hands with gap straights, the one with the larger gap ranks higher. If the gap sizes are equal, the hand with the highest card ranks higher.

3. Between hands with no gap straight, the hand whose cards have the highest sum ranks higher. If the sums are equal, the hand with the highest card outranks the other.

The guests played several hands without getting many gap straights, but then had a hand in which all seven players ended up with gap straights after just three pairs of cards were exchanged. From the following clues, can you determine what three cards each player was dealt, what card exchanges were made, and how the players' hands ranked after the exchanges?

1. The 1, 2, and 3 were dealt to Greg, Logan, and Olivia, respectively.

2. The 19, 20, and 21 were dealt to Greg, Taylor, and Emma, respectively.

3. The 5 and 7 were dealt to James and Taylor, respectively.

4. James didn't trade away his lowest or highest card.

5. The three cards dealt to Abby had a sum of 50.

6. Two of the cards dealt to Logan had a product of 24.

7. Two players were dealt a gap straight.

8. Three exchanges were made: Abby exchanged a card for one of Olivia's cards, James and Taylor similarly exchanged a card, and Emma and Greg also exchanged a card. After these three exchanges, everyone had a gap straight.

Mini Mahjong

Taylor is developing a simple game that uses mahjong tiles in a different way from the regular game. The other six guests agree to test the game, if for no other reason than they like the look of the tiles. For a six-player game, only 66 tiles from a mahjong set are used: three of each of the four winds (North, East, South, and West), and two each of the 27 suit tiles, which come in three suits (Bamboos, Dots, and Characters) with numerical values of 1 through 9.

The tiles are mixed face-down, and 11 are dealt to each player. Players look at their tiles, then choose three to pass to another player. In the first round, players pass tiles to the player on their left. In the second round, players pass tiles to the player directly across from them. In the third round, players pass tiles to the player on their right. After that, the sequence repeats: pass left, pass across, pass right.

The object is to be the first to collect four pairs of identical tiles, such as two 5's of bamboo (not two 5's of different suits) or two North winds. Once any player collects four pairs, the hand is over. It is possible for more than one player to achieve this on the same turn. An agreed-upon number of hands is played, after which the player with the most total points wins.

For each pair collected, players score 10 points plus the face values of the two tiles. For example, a pair of 3 of dots would earn $10 + 3 + 3 = 16$ points. Wind cards have a face value of zero but a pair of them still earns 10 points. A player who collects four pairs also adds, as a bonus, 25 points plus the face value of his or her remaining three tiles. More than one player can collect this bonus if they all collect their fourth pair on the same turn. The players with fewer than four pairs subtract the face value of their unpaired tiles from their scores. Negative scores are possible. Special bonuses can be earned for collecting four pairs of wind cards (100 points) or four pairs of all the same suit (50 points).

From the following observations recorded by Taylor as Abby, Emma, Greg, James, Logan, and Olivia played a hand, can you determine each player's scores and the denominations of all their pairs?

1. The only player who collected four pairs was tied for the second-highest score.

2. One player had unpaired tiles with a total face value of zero.

3. The player who scored −3 was the only one with a negative score and the only one with just one pair. The sum of the other five players' scores was 282.

4. The player with one pair had unpaired tiles with a face value one point less than the unpaired tiles of a player with two pairs, whose unpaired tiles were exactly five times the value of the unpaired tiles of the player with the best score.

5. Abby and Olivia, who each had three pairs, tied for the highest total face value of paired tiles. Neither of them had the highest score, although one did tie for the second-highest score.

6. Olivia had unpaired tiles with a face value double that of the player with the highest score, and Abby's unpaired tiles were one point less than Olivia's.

7. Emma had a higher score than James but a lower score than Logan.

8. The high scorer, who was not Logan, had no two pairs of matching denominations.

9. Three different players had South wind tiles.

The Missing Medallion

The premise of this mystery penned by the Montagues is that a rare medallion struck in silver after the American Revolution to commemorate the British surrender at Yorktown disappeared from a display case in the lounge sometime between 12:30 P.M. and 3:30 P.M. Being small and easy to hide, the medallion was immediately hidden by the thief, who wanted to avoid being caught with it and hoped to remove it from the premises at a later time.

Based on movements of guests around the house during this time, the medallion is hidden in one of four places: the library, the pantry, the sitting room, or the small game room. From the statements of the Montagues, staff, and guest, can you determine which guest is the thief and where the medallion is hidden?

Statements by the Montagues:

1. Gordon: All the guests claim to have been in only the dining room, library, sitting room, or small game room between 12:30 and 3:30. None of them left the mansion or went to the guest wing during those hours. The theft could not have been done by someone who was with another guest at the time, nor could the medallion have been hidden in a room when another guest was present there.

2. Nina: There is only one thief. No one will lie about the room they were in during a given hour or lie about anyone else's location, although the guilty party won't admit having left a room to steal or hide the medallion.

Statements by the staff:

3. Alistair: From 12:30 to 1:30, two guests were present in each of three different rooms, one of which was the library. Of these six guests, only one of the two who had been in the dining room stayed another hour in the same room; the other five all changed rooms at 1:30.

4. Charlotte: One guest was in the library for two consecutive hours, and never left the library during that time.

5. Evelyn: Since I was in the kitchen from 12:30 to 2:30, no one could have entered the pantry during that time except from the dining room.

6. Grant: As of 1:30, the medallion was not hidden in the small game room.

7. Lyle: Emma was in the dining room from 1:30 to 2:30.

8. Sandy: From 1:30 to 2:30, Greg was in the room where Emma had been from 12:30 to 1:30, and Greg changed rooms at 2:30.

Statements by the guests:

9. Abby: Three guests were in the small game room from 1:30 to 2:30.

10. Emma: I was in the sitting room from 2:30 to 3:30 with two other guests.

11. Greg: I was in the sitting room with James from 12:30 to 1:30.

12. James: I was in the small game room from 2:30 to 3:30 with just one other guest. That guest had been in the library from 12:30 to 1:30.

13. Logan: I was in the sitting room from 1:30 to 3:30.

14. Olivia: I was in the dining room from 12:30 to 1:30 only.

15. Taylor: Between 12:30 and 3:30, I was never in the dining room or library.

	12:30–1:30				1:30–2:30				2:30–3:30			
	DR	Lib	SR	SGR	DR	Lib	SR	SGR	DR	Lib	SR	SGR
Abby												
Emma												
Greg												
James												
Logan												
Olivia												
Taylor												

Book Exchange

All the guests are avid readers, and over the course of the summer they each lent books they had finished to other guests. From the following clues, can you determine who lent which books to whom?

1. Abby, Emma, Greg, James, Logan, Olivia, and Taylor each own two of the following books: *First Family, Second Fiddle, Third Degree, Fourth Estate, Fifth Avenue, Sixth Sense, Seventh Heaven, Eighth Wonder, Ninth Inning, 10th Street, 11th Hour, 12th Day, 13th Floor, 14th Amendment.*

2. Each guest lent exactly two books to other guests, but no one lent two books to the same guest or borrowed two books from the same guest.

3. Emma and James borrowed books from one another, and Logan and Taylor borrowed books from one another; the books were *Second Fiddle, Seventh Heaven, 10th Street,* and *12th Day.* No other guests borrowed a book from someone to whom they lent a book.

4. In addition to the books borrowed from one another, Emma, James, Logan, and Taylor borrowed two books from Greg and one each from James and Olivia, in some combination.

5. In addition to the books lent to one another, Emma, James, Logan, and Taylor lent two books to Abby and one each to Olivia and Taylor.

6. *First Family, 13th Floor,* and *14th Amendment* are owned by Greg, James, and Olivia, in some combination. Greg, James, and Taylor each borrowed one of them.

7. *Third Degree, Fourth Estate, Fifth Avenue,* and *Sixth Sense* are owned by Abby, Greg, Olivia, and Taylor in some combination, and were borrowed by Abby, Emma, Greg, and Logan, in some combination.

8. One guest owns *Seventh Heaven* and *11th Hour,* and another owns *Second Fiddle* and *Ninth Inning.*

9. One guest borrowed *Second Fiddle* and *13th Floor,* and another guest borrowed *Third Degree* and *10th Street.*

10. James and Logan each borrowed a book from the same guest.

11. *Fifth Avenue* was borrowed by the person who lent *Sixth Sense* to Greg.

12. Emma borrowed *10th Street* from the person who lent *First Family.*

13. Logan did not lend *Second Fiddle* or *Ninth Inning,* and Olivia did not lend *Fourth Estate.*

	book owner							book borrower						
	Abby	Emma	Greg	James	Logan	Olivia	Taylor	Abby	Emma	Greg	James	Logan	Olivia	Taylor
First Family														
Second Fiddle														
Third Degree														
Fourth Estate														
Fifth Avenue														
Sixth Sense														
Seventh Heaven														
Eighth Wonder														
Ninth Inning														
10th Street														
11th Hour														
12th Day														
13th Floor														
14th Amendment														
Abby	X						
Emma		X					
Greg			X				
James				X			
Logan					X		
Olivia						X	
Taylor							X

book borrower

Attack in the Foyer

In this mystery puzzle, the seven guests (Abby, Emma, Greg, James, Logan, Olivia, and Taylor) as well as cabin cruiser and helicopter pilot Nolan, are assuming the roles of visitors from a small town, all of whom have known one another for years and may harbor dark secrets. Each guest is playing the part of someone with a different profession, and Nolan is playing the role of a reporter who writes about town gossip.

From the statements below, can you determine which profession and which possible reason for the attack go with each guest, and determine who the attempted murderer is?

Statements by the Montagues:

1. Gordon: In the middle of the afternoon on Saturday, as Nolan walked out of the library into the foyer, a vase was dropped from the second-floor balcony outside the small game room. It hit Nolan and broke, but fortunately only dazed him. One of the guests was attempting to kill him, and the reason was anger, blackmail, fear, greed, insanity, jealousy, or revenge. Each guest had exactly one of these possible reasons for attacking Nolan, and no two guests had the same possible reason.

2. Nina Montague: Each guest has one of the following occupations: glazier, herpetologist, illustrator, jeweler, librarian, machinist, naturalist. No two have the same occupation. As usual, only the guilty guest may make a false statement.

Statements by the staff:

3. Alistair: James, Olivia, and Taylor have the occupations herpetologist, jeweler, and librarian, in some combination.

4. Charlotte: Emma, James, and Logan have anger, fear, and revenge as their possible motives, in some combination.

5. Evelyn: The possible reasons the glazier, illustrator, and librarian might have attacked are greed, insanity, and jealousy, in some combination.

6. Grant: The machinist's possible motive is not revenge.

7. Lyle: The naturalist's possible motive is not revenge.

8. Sandy: Taylor's possible motive is not blackmail.

Statements by the guests:

9. Abby: The jeweler's possible motive is not revenge.

10. Emma: My possible motive is not anger.

11. Greg: My possible motive is not jealousy.

12. James: The naturalist's possible motive is not fear.

13. Logan: My possible motive is either fear or revenge.

14. Olivia: Neither Abby nor the illustrator would have attacked for the reason of insanity.

15. Taylor: Logan is not the naturalist.

	glazier	herpetologist	illustrator	jeweler	librarian	machinist	naturalist	anger	blackmail	fear	greed	insanity	jealousy	revenge
Abby														
Emma														
Greg														
James														
Logan														
Olivia														
Taylor														
anger							
blackmail							
fear							
greed							
insanity							
jealousy							
revenge							

Tropical Taste Test

For an afternoon snack, Chef Evelyn has prepared samples of the edible portions of 10 tropical fruits, some of which are unusual. The guests are given a list of the fruits: cherimoya, dragon fruit, guava, lychee, mango, papaya, passion fruit, persimmon, rambutan, and star fruit. Each guest samples each fruit and tries to identify it from its look and taste. Guests score one point for each correctly identified fruit, and each fruit earns a score equal to the number of guests who correctly identified it. The results of the test, as usual, become the basis for a puzzle by the Montagues.

From the following clues, can you determine which fruits were correctly identified by each guest?

1. Of the 10 tastings made by each of the seven guests, a total of 40 correct identifications were made.

2. No two guests had the same score.

3. Each fruit had the same score as exactly one other fruit, and two fruits were identified by all seven guests.

4. Every fruit was identified by at least one guest, but no guest identified all 10 fruits.

5. No fruit had a score equal to the score of the lowest-scoring guest.

6. Taylor's score was two more than double Abby's score.

7. Abby scored higher than Logan.

8. James ended up with the same score as guava.

9. Olivia and Taylor identified the same fruits with three exceptions: Olivia identified cherimoya and lychee while Taylor did not, and Taylor identified rambutan, which Olivia did not.

10. Emma and James identified cherimoya.

11. Mango's score is equal to the sum of the scores of cherimoya and star fruit.

12. Papaya's score is equal to the sum of the scores of dragon fruit and passion fruit.

13. Every guest either identified both persimmon and star fruit or failed to identify both persimmon and star fruit, with one exception: Greg identified persimmon but not star fruit.

14. Cherimoya and dragon fruit had the same score.

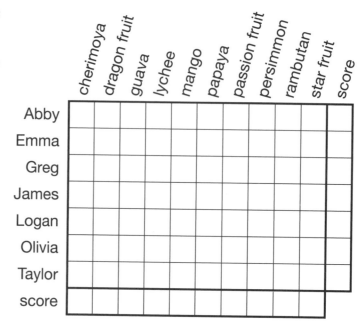

Revelation

Two hours after the other regular guests departed for the last time this season, you knock on the door to Gordon Montague's private study.

"Ah, the winner of this season's mystery solving prize. I thought you had left with the others, Taylor."

"No, I promised you an explanation by the end of this weekend. I've made up a little puzzle featuring the names of six young people whom you've met this summer. One of them is the client I told you about—the one responsible for the messages. That person, who is waiting downstairs with Nina, is the answer to this puzzle: Whose three statements can all be true?"

Cheryl
1. Siobhan's third statement is false.
2. Either Siobhan's or Vince's first statement is true, or both.
3. Rory's second statement is true.

Isabel
1. Either Rory's or Zach's second statement is true, or both.
2. Cheryl's third statement is true.
3. Rory's first statement is true.

Vince
1. Siobhan's second statement is false.
2. Isabel's second statement is false.
3. Cheryl's second statement is false.

Rory
1. Vince's third statement is true.
2. Isabel's third statement is false.
3. Cheryl's third statement is false.

Siobhan
1. Vince's second statement is false.
2. Either Zach's first or third statement is true, or both.
3. Isabel's second statement is false.

Zach
1. Cheryl's third statement is true.
2. Siobhan's third statement is true.
3. Rory's third statement is true.

(An epilogue follows the answer to this puzzle.)

ANSWERS AND EXPLANATIONS

Note: Throughout these answers, numbered statements in the puzzles are referred to as "clues."

Weekend 1

Puzzle 1.1: Key Deductions

Starting with box 2 leads to boxes 5, 11, 9, 10, and 6, which is the sequence that uses the most keys, so the prize is in box 6. Starting with box 1 leads to boxes 4, 12, and 8. Starting with box 3 leads only to box 7.

Box 4 must contain the key to box 12 since that key is found nowhere else. Since box 4 contains the key to box 12, box 12 cannot contain the key to box 4, since there would then be no way to open either box. Therefore, box 12 contains the key to box 8, which means that box 3 contains the key to box 7 and box 11 contains the key to box 9, which contains the key to box 10.

If box 10 contained the key to box 11, the keys to boxes 9, 10, and 11 would all be within those same three boxes, and no other box would have a key to any of them. Therefore, box 10 contains the key to box 6 and box 2 contains the key to box 5. Since box 12 does not contain the key to box 4, box 1 does. The key to box 11 must be in box 5, and boxes 6, 7, and 8 have no keys. In summary:

Box 1 contains the key to box 4.
Box 2 contains the key to box 5.
Box 3 contains the key to box 7.
Box 4 contains the key to box 12.
Box 5 contains the key to box 11.
Box 6 contains the prize.
Box 7 is empty.
Box 8 is empty.
Box 9 contains the key to box 10.
Box 10 contains the key to box 6.
Box 11 contains the key to box 9.
Box 12 contains the key to box 8.

Puzzle 1.2: The New Guests

Abby is the physicist, the Wildcat, and the Ultimate enthusiast.
Emma is the philosophy student, the Panther, and the tennis enthusiast.
Greg is the psychology student, the Cougar, and the golf enthusiast.
James is the historian, the Lion, and the curling enthusiast.
Logan is the economics student, the Bear, and the lacrosse enthusiast.
Olivia is the music student, the Tiger, and the rugby enthusiast.
Taylor is the mathematician, the Bulldog, and the volleyball enthusiast.

From clue 3, the students of economics, history, mathematics, and music are James, Logan, Olivia, and Taylor, in some combination. Similarly, the guests and sports not named in clue 4 must go together, as must the unnamed subjects and school nicknames in clue 5 and the unnamed sports and nicknames in clue 6.

Since Abby, Emma, and Greg are not the lacrosse, rugby, or volleyball enthusiasts, the students of philosophy, physics, and psychology do not go with any of these sports.

Clue 7 eliminates all pairings of golf, James, and music, and also means that none of the students of economics, history, and mathematics is the golf enthusiast (we already knew that Logan, Olivia, and Taylor weren't golf enthusiasts), nor is the Wildcat.

Clue 8 eliminates all pairings of volleyball, Olivia, economics, and Wildcats, and means that the Wildcat's sport is Ultimate. Olivia's sport is not golf or volleyball and so she is not the Bulldog or Cougar, and neither is James. Being the Wildcat, the Ultimate enthusiast's only possible fields of study are history and physics, and neither Logan nor Taylor (neither of whom is the Ultimate enthusiast) is the Wildcat.

Since neither the Bear nor the Panther can be the student of history, mathematics, or music (clues 5 and 9), which are Olivia's only possible fields, Olivia is not the Bear or Panther. None of James, Logan, or Taylor is the Panther.

Clue 10 rules out lacrosse, rugby, and tennis for the history student, which also rules out history as Olivia's field of study. Olivia cannot be the Lion, which is not a possible nickname for the mathematics or music student; so Olivia is the Tiger, which means that the Tiger is not the philosophy or psychology student and the Tiger's sport is not curling or tennis.

Clue 11 eliminates all pairings of Abby, the Bear, and the curling and tennis enthusiasts, and rules out Taylor as the Bear. Since Abby can only be the golf or Ultimate enthusiast, she cannot be the Lion or Panther. Emma is not the Bear, which has no sports interest in common with her. For the same reason, neither Greg nor James is the Bear, so Logan is. Therefore Logan's sport is not volleyball, and so Taylor's must be, which means that Taylor is not the Lion. Taylor is the Bulldog or Cougar, who can only be students of mathematics, music, philosophy, or psychology; but the only one of these fields that Taylor can be in is mathematics (clues 3 and 12). Therefore, Taylor is the mathematician, as well as the Bulldog (clue 13), and by elimination Olivia the Tiger is the student of music, and the Cougar's sport is golf.

The Bear is either the economist or physicist, and since Logan is not the physicist, Logan is the economist and has lacrosse as his sport (clue 14). James is the student of history, and rugby is the sport of Olivia the Tiger.

Because the Cougar's sport is golf, the Cougar cannot be the student of philosophy (clue 15) and must instead be the student of psychology, which means that the Panther is the student of philosophy. Since Greg is not the Panther (clue 13), Emma is, and her sport is either curling or tennis.

Since Abby is not the psychologist (clue 12), she is the physicist. Greg is the student of psychology and is the Cougar. By elimination, James is the Lion, Abby is the Wildcat and Ultimate enthusiast, and curling is the sport of the history student (James). Tennis is the sport of Emma, the philosophy student.

Puzzle 1.3: Murder in the Game Alcove

Emma is the killer. The corporate titles of and luxury items owned by each guest are as follows:
Abby is vice president of research and owns the van Gogh painting.
Emma is comptroller and owns a ski chalet.
Greg is vice president of marketing and owns a yacht.
James is treasurer and owns a vintage Aston Martin automobile.
Logan is secretary and owns a South Pacific island.
Olivia is president and owns an airplane.
Taylor is CEO and owns an inverted Jenny postage stamp.

From the statements of Lyle and Abby, the owner of the van Gogh is either the vice president of research or the treasurer. The van Gogh owner cannot be James, Olivia, or Taylor (Logan's statement) nor either Greg or Logan (Emma's statement, which encompasses both job titles that could own the van Gogh).

From Lyle's and Olivia's statements, the Aston Martin is not owned by the CEO, president, or vice president of research. From Abby's statement, the Aston Martin is not owned by the vice president of marketing, comptroller, or secretary. By elimination, the Aston Martin is owned by the treasurer, which means that the vice president of research owns the van Gogh.

The CEO and president own the airplane and the inverted Jenny in some combination (per Abby's statement and the already matched items). Since neither Greg nor Logan owns either of these items (Logan's statement), neither of them is CEO or president. By elimination (from Emma's and Greg's statements), Greg is the vice president of marketing, and Logan is the secretary. Because James does not own the island, ski chalet, or yacht (Logan's statement), he is not the comptroller. Since James does not own the van Gogh, he is not the vice president of research. He isn't the CEO or president either (he was in the lounge when they were in the library, per his and Lyle's statements), so he must be the treasurer, who owns the Aston Martin.

Taylor does not own an airplane (Taylor's statement), so per Logan's statement, Olivia must, and Taylor owns the inverted Jenny. Since Taylor did not speak with Lyle, Olivia is president and Taylor is CEO.

From his statement, Greg does not own an island. From Grant's statement, Emma does not own an island or a yacht.

Per Taylor's statement, Emma was not in the lounge between 4:30 and 5, so she does not own the van Gogh, and by elimination Abby does, and is the vice president of research. By elimination, Emma is the comptroller and owns a ski chalet, Greg owns a yacht, and Logan owns an island.

At the time of the murder, Greg and Logan were not in the mansion (Grant's statement), James was in the library (James's statement), and Abby, Olivia, and Taylor were in the lounge (Lyle's statement). Only Emma had the opportunity to kill the bookkeeper, who she was afraid was planning to confess their embezzlement scheme to the company.

Weekend 2

Puzzle 2.1: Film Festival

The number of votes each film received is shown in parentheses after its title.

Abby brought in *Blue Jasmine* (2), *Blue Valentine* (3), and *Blue Velvet* (2).
Emma brought in *Fierce People* (1), *Funny People* (0), and *Ordinary People* (6).
Greg brought in *Jupiter Ascending* (1), *Mars Attacks!* (3), and *Saturn 3* (3); and he broke the tie in favor of Mars Attacks!.
James brought in *BUtterfield 8* (1), *Jennifer 8* (2), and *Super 8* (4).
Logan brought in *August Rush* (4), *September Dawn* (0), and *October Sky* (3).
Olivia brought in *Elephant Walk* (1), *Horse Feathers* (1), and *Whale Rider* (5).
Taylor brought in *Bully* (0), *Sully* (2), and *Tully* (5).

The possible ways to distribute seven votes among three films are 7-0-0, 6-1-0, 5-1-1, 5-2-0, 4-2-1, 4-3-0, 3-3-1, and 3-2-2. From clue 1, every possible combination of votes except 7-0-0 was received by one set of films.

The two films mentioned in clue 5 were in categories with 4-3-0, 3-3-1, or 3-2-2 vote distributions (clue 3). Since the only vote total in common between any two of these is 3, *Blue Valentine* and *Mars Attacks!* each received three votes.

The distribution of *Blue* films is either 4-3-0, 3-3-1, or 3-2-2, and the possible distributions of films beginning with an animal and *-ully* films are 6-1-0, 5-1-1, 5-2-0, or 4-2-1 (clue 3). For *Tully* and *Whale Rider* to have the same number of votes and for *Tully* to have finished first in its group (clue 6), each must have received five votes. *Sully* finished second by itself in its category, so the *-ully* films can't be distributed 5-1-1 or *Sully* would be tied for second, so they're 5-2-0 and *Sully* received two votes and *Bully* got no votes. The animal films, then, are the 5-1-1 category, so *Elephant Walk* and *Horse Feathers* got one vote apiece. Since *Blue Velvet* got two votes (the same as Sully, per clue 6), *Blue Jasmine* got the remaining two votes, and films beginning with *Blue* had a vote distribution of 3-2-2.

At least one film brought by Abby, James, and Taylor received two votes (clue 2). Abby's films' votes were not distributed 5-2-0, since that was the voting for the *-ully* films she did not bring (clue 6), nor were her films' votes distributed 4-2-1, since (per clue 4) her films were not in the categories "ends in 8" or "ends in *People*," the only possibilities for the 4-2-1 films (the others are eliminated by clue 3). Her films' vote distribution was therefore 3-2-2, and so she brought in the *Blue* films. Taylor's vote distribution was therefore either 5-2-0 or 4-2-1, neither of which is the group that begins with an animal or planet; Taylor also didn't bring the sets in clue 4, so Taylor brought in *Bully*, *Sully*, and *Tully* and had the vote distribution 5-2-0. By elimination, James had the vote distribution 4-2-1.

Since neither Greg nor Olivia brought in the films ending in 8 or *People* (clue 4), neither has the 6-1-0 vote distribution. Since Emma and Logan did not bring in films beginning with an animal (clue 4 again), neither had the 5-1-1 vote distribution.

From clue 8, since the films ending in *People* had a vote distribution of either 6-1-0 or 4-2-1, *Jupiter Ascending* received either $1 + 0 = 1$ vote or $2 + 1 = 3$ votes. In either case, since *Mars Attacks!* received 3 votes, films that begin with a planet had the vote distribution 3-3-1, and so films beginning with a month had the distribution 4-3-0. Since *October Sky* finished below *August Rush* (clue 9) but had more than *Jupiter Ascending* (clue 8), it must have had 3 votes, and so *Jupiter Ascending* received only 1 vote, which means that *Saturn 3* received 3 votes. Therefore, films ending in *People* had the vote distribution 6-1-0 (clue 8) and films ending in 8 had the distribution 4-2-1 and were James's. *Fierce People* had one vote and *Funny People* had none, leaving *Ordinary People* with six votes.

From clue 7, Emma and Olivia must have had vote distributions of 6-1-0 and 5-1-1 respectively, and Logan must have had 4-3-0; by elimination, Greg's was 3-3-1. Clue 9 resolves the remaining unknown vote totals, and Clue 10 breaks the tie between *Mars Attacks!* and *Saturn 3* in favor of the former.

Puzzle 2.2: Bookshelf

The order in which guest rearranged the books was: Logan, Abby, Emma, James, Taylor, Greg, Olivia.

If the books are labeled A through G, the left-to-right order changed as follows after each borrowing and replacement:

ABCDEFG (starting order)
BACDEFG
GACDEFB
GACFBDE
GDCFBAE
GCDFBAE
GCEDFBA
GFEDCBA

Consider the sequences of book moves by the guests that will get certain books from their starting locations to their destinations.

The center book (D) ends up in its starting position despite moving out of it when Emma or Greg borrows books. Emma's turn would move book D two spaces to the right, while Greg's moving the last book to the third position would move book D one space to the right. If Emma's turn came before Greg's, book D could only have gotten back to the middle by moving to the second, third, and fourth positions via the moves of James, Taylor, and Greg, in that order. If Greg's turn came before Emma's, book D could only have gotten back to the middle by moving to the second, sixth, and fourth positions via the moves of Olivia, James, and Emma, in that order. This leaves possible sequences of Emma-James-Taylor-Greg, with Olivia's turn's position to be determined, and Greg-Olivia-James-Emma, with Taylor's turn's position still to be determined. In either case, the timing of the sequence Logan-Abby (known from Abby's statement) is also still to be determined.

Now consider how book F moves from the sixth to the second position. The first time it changes positions must be when Emma, James, or Greg borrows books. For book D to end up in the fourth position, either Emma or Greg took a turn before James did, and so the first time book F moved out of sixth position was either when Emma or Greg borrowed books. If Emma borrowed books before Greg, book F could have moved to the fourth, fifth, and second positions via turns of Emma, Greg, and Olivia, in that order. If Greg borrowed books before Emma, book F could have moved to the seventh, fifth, and second positions via turns of Greg, Emma, and Olivia, in that order. (It can't have moved to the seventh, first, and second positions via the turns of Greg, Abby, and Logan because Logan's turn did not follow Abby's.) Neither of these is compatible with the sequence Greg-Olivia-James-Emma, which means that Emma-James-Taylor-Greg is the correct sequence, and Olivia's turn must come later than Greg's.

Since Abby's turn came just after Logan's, she must have moved book G from the seventh position to the first position. This must have happened just before Emma's turn, because book G would never again have been in the seventh position during the sequence of turns Emma-James-Taylor-Greg-Olivia. (Emma's turn would have moved it to the fifth position, and later Greg's turn would have moved it to the sixth position.)

Puzzle 2.3: Six, Zero

The secret word is ISLAND.

From Emma's guess, at most three of the letters AEIN are in the secret word. Logan's guess contains five matches, and his guess includes the letters AEIN. Three of those letters plus the other two (LS) make five, so L and S must be in the word and three of AEIN are as well. Abby's guess contains two matches, one of which is L; the other must be A or E (which also means that either A or E is not a match). We now know ILNS are four matches and A or E is the fifth.

In James's guess I and L account for two matches and A or E account for the third, so D or T is the fourth. But the letters AEIN account for all the matches in Emma's guess, so T can't be a match, which means D is. Now DILNS and either A or E account for all six letters. Those letters don't include O or R, so Greg's four matches include the A in SAILOR and we now know the six letters are ADILNS.

Two letters in SALINE are in the correct position, but they are not S or A (since SAILOR has no letters in the correct position).

If the letter I is in the correct position, then neither A nor I in INTAKE is in the correct position, contrary to Taylor's response to INTAKE. Therefore, I in SALINE is not in the correct position, and L and N must be. In INTAKE, therefore, since N is not in the correct position, both I and A must be. This means that D and S fit in the blanks in the word I _ L A N _ , and since IDLANS is not in any dictionary, ISLAND is the secret word.

Puzzle 2.4: Synchronized Walking

Abby's route was old well → windmill → bridge → pond.
Cheryl's route was boathouse → mansion → bridge → pond → old well → windmill.
Emma's route was lighthouse → boathouse → mansion → bridge → windmill.
Greg's route was bridge → windmill → old well → sea caves.
James's route was windmill → bridge → pond → old well → Lookout Point.
Logan's route was pond → old well → windmill → bridge.
Nolan's route was mansion → bridge → windmill → old well.
Olivia's route was Lookout Point → boathouse → mansion → bridge.
Taylor's route was sea caves → old well → pond → bridge → mansion → boathouse → lighthouse.

There are only two ways to get to the bridge in 30 minutes: starting at the windmill (30 minutes to the bridge, directly) and starting at the sea caves (30 minutes via the old well and pond). James and Taylor took those routes (clue 4) and one of them continued in the direction the other one came from. Whoever started at the sea caves can't have continued to the windmill, because then it's impossible for that route to take 65 minutes exactly. So the person who started at the windmill continued toward the pond and old well, and must have walked from there to Lookout Point to finish in 65 minutes. The other person, therefore, continued to the mansion and followed the only 65-minute route possible from there, to the boathouse and lighthouse. Since we know Taylor passed by the mansion (clue 5), Taylor is the one who started at the sea caves and James started at the windmill.

At least four people besides James passed the windmill at different times (clue 6). There are four possible times to pass the windmill: starting at the old well (25 minutes), starting at the bridge (30 minutes), starting 10 minutes from the old well (35 minutes), and starting 10 minutes from the bridge (40 minutes). (You can also get from Lookout Point to the windmill in 40 minutes, but then it takes longer than 65 minutes total to get to the next map location, so that's impossible.) Per the order in clue 6, Abby started at the old well and Greg started at the bridge; each continued in the direction they were walking (55 minutes) and walked 10 more minutes in some direction. Logan started 10 minutes away from the old well; we know Taylor started at the sea caves, so Logan must have started at the pond, walked past the old well and windmill, and ended at the bridge. Since Greg started at the bridge, he can't have finished at the pond (clue 3), so the last part of his route must have been to the sea caves. Nolan started 10 minutes from the bridge, but didn't start at the pond (since Logan started there), so he started at the mansion, walked past the bridge and windmill, and ended at the old well. Abby's route, therefore, didn't end at the mansion (clue 3), so the last path she took was the one to the pond.

Taylor's path took 40 minutes to reach the mansion. Cheryl and Emma passed the mansion before that, and Olivia passed it after that (clue 5), starting from the three remaining locations, in some order: the lighthouse, boathouse, and Lookout Point. Of those, the boathouse and lighthouse are the two starting points that can get there sooner than 40 minutes. Cheryl started from the boathouse (10 minutes to the mansion, directly) and Emma started from the lighthouse (25 minutes to the mansion via the boathouse). Cheryl's path must have continued to the bridge; from there she took a route that takes 45 more minutes, and there is only one: walking past the pond and old well and finishing at the windmill. Emma also continued to the bridge; from there the rest of her route must have taken 30 minutes. That could take her either to the windmill (directly) or to the sea caves (via the pond and old well). But Taylor walked from the sea caves to the lighthouse, so Emma can't have walked from the lighthouse to the sea caves (clue 3), and instead she walked to the windmill.

That leaves Olivia starting at Lookout Point. One of the two possible routes she could have taken to the mansion (via the old well, pond, and bridge) has no possible continuation lasting 65 minutes in total. She therefore walks to the mansion via the boathouse and finishes her route at the bridge.

Weekend 3

Puzzle 3.1: Murder at the Embassy

The assassin is Taylor, who uses the code name Kylin and is from Halcyonna.
Abby, code name Chimaera from Shalomar, passed along information to Emma, code name Basilisk from Elysia.
Greg, code name Griffin from Wyvernia, received information from Olivia, code name Dragon from Ulteria.
James, code name Unicorn from Atlantea, received information from Logan, code name Sphinx from Lemuria.

Since only three guests say they received information, one of the four guests claiming to have passed on information to another guest is lying and must be guilty. The statements of the other three guests—Emma, Greg, and James—can therefore be trusted (Gordon's statement). Since they all received information, none of them can be from Lemuria, Shalomar, or Ulteria.

From Charlotte's statement, the spies from Elysia, Lemuria, Shalomar, and Ulteria must be the Basilisk, the Chimaera, the Dragon, and the Sphinx, in some combination.

From Evelyn's statement, Logan, the Kylin, and the spy from Wyvernia are three different people, as are the combinations Taylor–Unicorn–Lemuria and James–Sphinx–Elysia. From Grant's statement, Abby, the Unicorn, and the spy from Ulteria are three different people, as are the combinations Olivia–Griffin–Atlantea and Greg–Dragon–Shalomar. Sandy's statement eliminates any combinations of Emma, Unicorn, and Wyvernia. By elimination, the Griffin is from Wyvernia.

By elimination, James is from Atlantea, Halcyonna, or Wyvernia, but since he truthfully states he is not from Wyvernia, he must be either the Kylin or Unicorn, who account for the spies from Atlantea and Halcyonna in some order. However, since he also truthfully says his code name is not Kylin, he is the Unicorn. James the Unicorn isn't from Wyvernia (since the Griffin is from there) so he isn't the person who stayed at the table the whole time in Evelyn's statement. The spy from Elysia can't be the one who stayed the whole time either, as there's no possible matching code name (James is the Unicorn and the Kylin is from Atlantea or Halcyonna), so the Sphinx was in all three groups. The Sphinx isn't

from Wyvernia, so is instead from Lemuria, and that spy's name is Logan. Since James truthfully reported receiving information from the Lemuria spy, Logan's statement is true, so James the Unicorn is the spy from Atlantea (and by elimination, the Kylin is from Halcyonna).

The person who sat at the table the whole time in Grant's statement isn't the Griffin (who is from Wyvernia, not Ulteria or Shalomar) or the spy from Atlantea (who is James, not Abby or Greg), so it's Olivia. She isn't the Unicorn, so she's the Dragon and is from Ulteria. Since Greg truthfully reported receiving information from the Ulteria spy, Olivia's statement is true, so Greg is from Wyvernia and is the Griffin.

The Unicorn and the spy from Ulteria are accounted for, so Abby is the one who left the table and returned in Grant's statement; therefore she is the spy from Shalomar. Since Emma truthfully reported receiving information from the Shalomar spy, Abby's statement is true, so Emma is from Elysia. By elimination, Taylor is the Kylin from Halcyonna, which means Taylor gave the false statement and is the murderer. Abby truthfully states she's not the Basilisk, so she can only be the Chimaera, making Emma the Basilisk.

Puzzle 3.2: A Day of Civiization

Emma played Thrace and finished first, despite a calamitous volcanic eruption.
Taylor played Crete and finished second, despite a calamitous epidemic.
Olivia played Illyria and finished third, despite a calamitous civil war.
James played Italy and finished fourth, despite calamitous attacks by pirates.
Abby played Egypt and finished fifth, despite a calamitous famine.
Greg played Assyria and finished sixth, in part due to a calamitous earthquake.
Logan played Babylon and finished seventh, very much on account of calamitous floods.

From clue 3: Greg, James, Logan, and Taylor played the nations whose calamities were earthquake, epidemic, flood, and piracy, in some combination.

From clue 4: Thrace did not finish sixth or seventh; Illyria did not finish first or second; the nation that suffered an epidemic did not finish first or seventh; and the nation that suffered an epidemic was not Illyria, Italy, or Thrace.

From clue 5: Greg did not finish first or seventh and did not play Egypt or the nation that suffered from flood; Egypt did not finish sixth or seventh and was not the nation that suffered from flood; and the nation that suffered from flood did not finish first or second.

From clue 6: Abby did not finish first or second and did not play Italy or the nation that suffered a civil war; Italy did not finish first or seventh and was not the nation that suffered a civil war; and the nation that suffered a civil war did not finish sixth or seventh.

From clue 7: James did not finish first, sixth, or seventh and did not play Assyria or Crete; Assyria did not finish first, second, or seventh; and Crete did not finish sixth or seventh.

From clue 8: Babylon did not finish first and was not the nation that suffered from famine; and the nation that suffered from famine did not finish seventh.

From clue 9: Olivia did not finish first and did not play the nation that suffered from a volcanic eruption; and the nation that suffered from a volcanic eruption did not finish seventh. Neither Abby nor Emma finished seventh, because their only possible calamities are ones that did not happen to the seventh-place nation.

From clue 10: Taylor did not finish sixth or seventh and was not the nation that suffered from earthquake or piracy; the nation that suffered from earthquake did not finish first or second; and the nation that suffered from piracy did not finish first or seventh. Neither Logan nor Taylor finished first, because their only possible calamities are ones that did not happen to the first-place nation. By elimination, Emma finished first and was not Assyria, Babylon, Illyria, or Italy, none of which finished first.

From clue 11: Since Abby was not first or second, Greg was not second or third; since Abby finished better than Greg, who was not seventh, she was not sixth; and since Olivia finished higher than Abby, Olivia was not fifth, sixth, or seventh. By elimination, Logan finished seventh, and by further elimination, Greg finished sixth. Since the nation with the volcano calamity finished ahead of Olivia (clue 9), that nation finished first, second, or third. Since Italy finished better than Abby (clue 6), Italy did not finish fifth or sixth. Logan's calamity was not epidemic or piracy, since neither of the nations with those calamities finished seventh.

From clue 12: Since Egypt was not sixth or seventh, Illyria was not fifth, sixth, or seventh and Crete was not fourth or fifth. Thrace finished at least two places better than Illyria (clue 4), and so did not finish third, fourth, or fifth. By elimination, Babylon finished seventh and was Logan. By further elimination, Assyria finished sixth and was Greg, and Egypt finished fifth (and so was not Emma or Olivia).

From clue 5, since Greg finished sixth, the nation with floods finished seventh and was Babylon/Logan. By elimination, Taylor's calamity was an epidemic.

The volcano was either Abby's or Emma's calamity; if Abby's, then Abby could only have finished third. Olivia would then have had to finish second (clue 11), but that would contradict clue 9 (Olivia finished behind the volcano nation). So Emma's nation had the volcanic eruption. By elimination, Abby's calamity was famine and Olivia's was civil war. Taylor was not Illyria, Italy, or Thrace, none of which had an epidemic (clue 4), and Olivia was not Italy, which had no civil war (clue 6), so by elimination James was Italy. Since Taylor finished better than Illyria (clue 4), Taylor did not finish fourth or fifth and so was not Egypt. By elimination, Taylor was Crete, and by further elimination, Abby was Egypt and finished fifth, Olivia was Illyria, and Emma was Thrace.

The calamities of earthquake and piracy go with Greg/Assyria and James/Italy, in some combination. The civil war nation (Olivia) finished second, third, or fourth; the epidemic nation (Taylor) finished second or third; and the famine nation (Abby) fifth.

From clue 10 and the fact that the seventh-place nation's calamity was flood, the piracy nation did not finish sixth. By elimination, the earthquake nation finished sixth and was Assyria. By elimination, piracy was the calamity of Italy. From clues 4 and 6, Olivia (Illyria, civil war) finished behind Taylor (epidemic) but ahead of James (Italy), so Taylor finished second, Olivia third, and James fourth.

Puzzle 3.3: The Memorable Mosaic

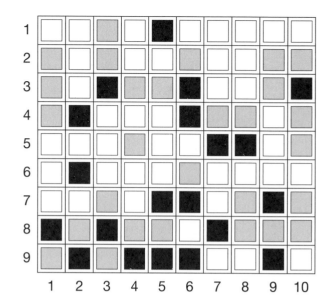

From clues 10 and 11, column 6 must contain at least four black tiles; if it only had three black tiles and no other column had more than two, the fact that three columns have just one black tile would mean a black tile total of at most 18, contradicting clue 1.

In column 6, the tiles in rows 7 and 9, which are known to match (clue 7), must be black. Otherwise, all four remaining spaces in that column would be black, contradicting the clue that states only one black tile is immediately above another in its column (clue 16).

Since the black tile in column 6 of row 9 must be the only black tile directly below a white tile in that column (clue 15), the row 2 and 6 tiles in that column are gray and the row 3 and 4 tiles are black.

Since only one row has no black tiles, rows 1 and 6 must each have one black and one gray tile (clues 2 and 3), and the column 2 tile in row 6 must be black. Rows 3, 4, 7, and 9 have black tiles in column 6. Row 8 must contain some black tiles, since there can be no more than three consecutive black tiles in row 9 (clue 12), so at least two of the first five spaces in row 9 must have gray tiles, and the tiles immediately above them are black (clue 8). Row 5 is known to have a black tile (clue 11). That leaves row 2 as the one with no black tiles, and so row 2 has five gray tiles.

The row with two gray and five black tiles mentioned in clue 9 cannot be 3, since that would mean that row 4 has two gray and four black tiles and that row 9 has an impossible nine black tiles (clues 4 and 5). Therefore, row 9 (the only other row with seven nonwhite tiles) has five black tiles, row 3 has four gray and three black, and row 4 has four gray and two black. The other rows with three black tiles mentioned in clue 6 must be 7 and 8 (not 5, which would cause black tiles to outnumber gray tiles in that row, contradicting clue 9). The row locations of 18 black tiles are now accounted for, which leaves the other two black tiles for row 5.

Row 9 contains five black tiles, but since it can't contain more than one set of adjacent black tiles (per clue 12, which describes three different rows) or four adjacent black tiles (also per clue 12), the tile in column 9 must be black, as is the row 7 column 9 tile (clue 7). Row 8 column 9 has a gray tile, per clue 8.

The pair of vertically adjacent black tiles mentioned in clue 16 are the row 3 and 4 tiles in column 6. In the southwest-to-northeast diagonal passing through the upper tile of that pair, the tile in row 5 column 4 could not be the only black tile in its column, since one of the two bottom tiles in that column must be black (clue 8). So the only other nonwhite tile on the diagonal (row 8 column 1) is black, and every other tile in column 1 is gray. Row 9 column 2 must be black (clue 14). That makes row 8 column 2 gray (clue 8), which in turn means row 4 column 2 must be black (clue 15). Since both row 4 black tiles are now accounted for, the remaining row 4 tiles in columns 7, 8, and 10 are gray. The column of three vertically adjacent gray tiles mentioned in clue 13 is already accounted for (in column 1), so the tile between rows 2 and 4 in column 10 must be black.

Looking back at row 9, the remaining gray tile can't go in column 4, or there would be two pairs of horizontally adjacent black tiles in that row, contradicting clue 12. So row 9 column 4 is black (and row 8 column 4 is gray per clue 8), and the gray tile is in column 3 or 5, which means row 9 is the row with three black tiles in a row (clue 12). Since row 3 isn't the row with three black tiles, it contains no horizontally adjacent black tiles (clue 12) and row 3's tiles in column 5 and column 9 are gray.

We already know neither of the pairs of adjacent black tiles can be in row 3 (clue 12). Row 8 is also impossible, because one of its remaining black tiles must be in column 3 or 5 (since one of those tiles must be black and the other gray), and the other is in column 7, 8, or 10. So the horizontally adjacent black tiles can only be in row 5 (columns 7 and 8) and row 7 (columns 5 and 6—not in the last three columns, because the third black tile in that row must be in column 3 or 5 due to clue 7). Row 9's column 5 tile is therefore black (clue 7), and column 3's tiles in rows 7 and 9 are gray. We've placed all the black tiles in rows 5 and 7, so the remaining tiles in each are gray, and in row 8 the tile in column 3 is black and the tile in column 5 is gray (clue 8).

In clue 16, we've already looked at one of the diagonals passing through row 3 column 6. There's only one black tile along the corresponding northwest-to-southeast diagonal, in row 5 column 8, so that's the only black tile in its column, and row 8 column 8 is gray. Somewhere there is a diagonal with three black tiles that are the only ones in their columns (clue 11), including one in row 5. The row 5 tile can't be the one in column 7; the southwest-to-northeast diagonal only has one other black tile in it, and the northwest-to-southeast contains only tiles that have other black tiles in the same column. So the diagonal includes row 5, column 8, and must be the southwest-to-northeast diagonal. Column 6 has four black tiles, so the other solo black tiles must be the ones in row 9 column 4 and row 3 column 10, which makes the remaining tiles in those columns gray. By elimination, row 3 column 3 and row 8 column 7 are black.

To account for all five pairs of adjacent gray tiles in columns mentioned in clue 13, the column 3 tile in row 1 must be gray, and the column 5 tile in row 1 is black.

Weekend 4

Puzzle 4.1: Three-Card Poker

Abby held the ♡Q, Emma the ◇K, Greg the ◇J, James the ♣J, Logan the ♡A, Olivia the ♣A, Taylor the ♡J, Nolan the ◇Q, and Cheryl the ♣10.

The cards held by Emma, Greg, and Nolan made a better hand than the cards held by Emma, Greg, and Abby, even though Abby and Nolan held cards of the same rank. Therefore, Nolan's card along with the cards of Emma and Greg must have formed a flush or straight flush, whereas the cards of Emma, Greg, and Abby did

not. Therefore, Emma, Greg, and Nolan held either ♣A, ♣J, and ♣10; ♡A, ♡Q, and ♡J; or ◇K, ◇Q, and ◇J, in some combination.

If the cards held by Emma, Greg, and Nolan were ♣A, ♣J, and ♣10, the hand formed by the cards of Abby, Emma, and Greg would have been AJ10 of two different suits. But in that case, whatever cards were held by Abby, Logan, and Taylor would have been a better hand. Why? The only 10 was held by either Emma or Greg (Abby can't have a 10 or Nolan would also have had one, per clue 1, but that's impossible), so Abby, Logan, and Taylor's cards couldn't include a 10. They also couldn't include a pair or form a straight, both of which outrank AJ10. But that leaves only AKJ and AQJ, which also outrank AJ10. Therefore, Emma, Greg, and Nolan did not hold ♣A, ♣J, and ♣10.

If the cards held by Emma, Greg, and Nolan were ♡A, ♡Q, and ♡J, the hand formed by the cards of Abby, Emma, and Greg would have been AQJ of two different suits. The cards held by Emma, Nolan, and Olivia had to outrank that hand without outranking a flush. If Emma, Nolan, and Olivia had a "nothing" hand, they must have held AKJ, with Olivia holding the king. Since Olivia's card was higher than Emma's (clue 3), Emma would have held the jack and Nolan the ace. That would have given Abby and Logan an ace and king respectively, in which case Abby, Logan, and Taylor's hand would have outranked Abby, Emma, and Greg's hand no matter what the third card was. If, instead, Emma, Nolan, and Olivia held a pair, Olivia and Nolan must have been the two who held it (since Olivia and Emma had cards of different ranks, per clue 3). But then the people in clues 1 and 2 would all have held the same rank of card, which is impossible. Emma, Greg, and Nolan, therefore, held a straight flush of ◇K, ◇Q, and ◇J in some order, and Abby, Emma, and Greg held a KQJ straight.

Emma, Nolan, and Olivia didn't hold three of a kind (clue 3), so to outrank Abby, Emma, and Greg, they must have held a higher straight, which could only be AKQ, which means Greg had the ◇J and Olivia an ace, which in turn means Logan also held an ace (clue 2). The only remaining hand that can outrank an AKQ straight is three of a kind, so Greg, James, and Taylor held three jacks (the only rank with three cards). Nolan didn't hold the king, because there wasn't another king for Abby to hold (clue 1), so Nolan had the ◇Q, Abby the ♡Q, and Emma the ◇K. James and Taylor held the ♡J and ♣J in some order, and Logan and Olivia held the ♡A and ♣A in some order.

By elimination, Cheryl had the ♣10. Logan, therefore, had the ♡A (clue 4) and Olivia the ♣A, and since Logan had a heart, James had the ♣J (clue 4) and Taylor the ♡J.

Puzzle 4.2: Murder in the Morning

Abby and James are the killers. They were alone with the victim in period 7, killed him, and hid his body in the crawlspace behind the sitting room closet so that it would not be discovered until the afternoon.

From clue 3, Abby, Emma, and Logan visited the small game room for more than one period and visited the screened porch for fewer than four periods; and the other five participants visited the screened porch for more than one period and the small game room for fewer than four periods. James, Logan, and Taylor each visited the art gallery for more than one period and the sitting room for fewer than four periods; and the other five participants visited the art gallery for fewer than four periods and the sitting room for more than one period.

From clue 4, the art gallery and screened porch must each have had three visitors who stayed for four periods, the sitting room two such visitors, and the small game room none. (No other combination consistent with clue 4 can account for all eight people's four-period stays.) Therefore, James, Logan, and Taylor each visited the art gallery for four periods, since they are the only three who could have. By elimination, since each participant made exactly one four-period visit, Greg, Nolan, and Olivia each visited the screened porch for four periods; and Abby and Emma's four-period visits were both to the sitting room.

Clue 5 identifies the three-period visits for four of the participants and, by elimination, pinpoints Abby's small game room visit and Greg's sitting room visit as each lasting two periods. (Clue 3 already eliminated the one-period option.) Greg spent just one period in the art gallery.

Clue 6 indicates Abby, Greg, Logan, and Taylor's rooms during the first and last periods, and between them they account for all the people starting and ending in those two rooms (clue 2). Abby was in the small game room during periods 1 and 2, and Greg was there during periods 1, 2, and 3. Abby's last four periods were in the sitting room.

From clues 7 and 9, James was in the art gallery during the first four periods. From clues 2 and 10, Emma and Nolan were on the screened porch during the first period, while Olivia was in the art gallery. The pair who was in the art gallery in the first period was in the screened porch in the last period, and vice versa.

Logan was in the small game room during the last three periods; Nolan was on the screened porch for the first four periods, and Olivia was there for the last four periods. Since Olivia's only possible one-period visit is the art gallery, and by elimination she was in the sitting room for two periods, in periods 5 and 6 (clue 8). She was therefore in the small game room during periods 2, 3, and 4.

From clue 3, Abby spent only one period on the screened porch, so she spent three in the art gallery. Taylor was not in the art gallery during period 4 (clue 7), and so Taylor's four-period stay there must begin in period 5 or 6. Either way, Taylor was in the art gallery during periods 6, 7, and 8.

Greg spent the last two periods in the sitting room, and he was in the art gallery in period 4 (clue 7), so his four periods on the screened porch began with period 5.

Since Greg, James, Nolan, and Olivia all changed rooms after period 4, no one else did (clue 11), and so both Abby and Logan were in the art gallery in both period 4 and period 5 (clue 7) and Emma was in the sitting room in periods 4, 5, and 6 (clue 8). Therefore, Emma's three-period stay in the small game room was in periods 7, 8, and 9, and her stay in the art gallery lasted only one period. By elimination she spent two periods on the screened porch. She was on the screened porch in period 2 and the sitting room in period 3. Taylor was in the same room during periods 4 and 5, so Taylor's art gallery visit could not have begun in period 5, and it therefore took place in periods 6 through 9, and Taylor only spent one period in the small game room (in period 10).

Nolan was in the sitting room in periods 5 and 6. If his small game room stay had been scheduled to be two or three periods, he would have been in the same room for periods 8 and 9, contradicting clue 11. Therefore he was in the small game room for one period. He also can't have been in the art gallery for three periods (clue 11), so his art gallery stay was two periods (9 and 10) and his sitting room stay was three periods (clue 3), leaving period 8 for his small game room visit.

Since Abby and Emma both changed rooms after period 2, Taylor did not (clue 11), and must have remained in the sitting room for the first three periods, followed by two periods on the screened porch. Logan also didn't change after period 2, so he didn't spend two periods in the sitting room and only spent one period there, and by elimination spent two periods on the screened porch.

Since James spent periods 5 and 6 in the small game room (clue 9) but spent more time on the screened porch (clue 3), he spent the last three periods on the screened porch and period 7 in the sitting room. Greg and Taylor changed rooms after period 3, so either Abby or Logan did, but not both (clue 11), so one of these two schedules is correct: Abby on the screened porch in period 3 and Logan on the screened porch in periods 6 and 7; or Abby on the screened porch in period 6 and Logan on the screened porch in periods 2 and 3. (The remaining periods are spent in the art gallery in either case.)

The pairs of guests who were alone with Nolan, or were scheduled to be, were Emma and Olivia in periods 5 and 6, Abby and James in period 7, Emma and Logan in period 8, and possibly Emma and Logan in period 2. One of those pairs is guilty.

At most two guests are lying. Olivia claims to have seen Nolan alive in period 6 and Abby and James claim to have seen him alive in period 7, so Nolan survived at least until period 7 or three people would have to be lying. Only two pairs of guests could have been alone with Nolan from period 7 onward: Abby and James in period 7 and Emma and Logan in period 8. (It's theoretically possible that if one person was alone with Nolan and a second person was alone in a different room, the second person could have slipped out unnoticed to join their accomplice, but two people were scheduled to be in each room in periods 9 and 10.) Emma and Logan can't both be guilty (clue 16), so Abby and James are the killers, and the murder took place in the sitting room during period 7. Since Logan isn't guilty, his statement is correct and he never saw Nolan, so he can't have been in the screened porch during periods 2 and 3, so Logan spent periods 2, 3, 4, and 5 in the art gallery and periods 6 and 7 in the screened porch. Abby spent period 3 in the screened porch and periods 4, 5, and 6 in the art gallery.

Puzzle 4.3: Full House

The rooms contain the following guests and sailing club members:

1A Greg	2A empty	3A Rory
1B Emma	2B Brent	3B Logan
1C Olivia	2C Derek	3C James
1D Phoebe	2D Zach	3D Siobhan
1E Taylor	2E Abby	3E Maria

Rory, Siobhan, and Logan are on the 3rd floor (clues 8, 9, and 10), as is James (clue 7). Zach is on the 2nd floor across from a sailing club member (clue 3) and Derek is also on the 2nd floor across from a regular guest (clue 4); those four guests occupy 2B, 2C, 2D, and 2E in some combination. Greg, Phoebe, and Emma are on the 1st floor (clues 8, 9, and 10). Olivia and Taylor are directly across from each other (clue 5); they can't be on the 3rd floor (four people on that floor are already accounted for) or the 2nd floor (if there were two regular guests on that floor, the second one would have to be in 2A, which isn't across from anyone), so they're on the 1st floor, and by elimination Abby is the only regular guest who can be on the 2nd floor, so she's the guest who's across from Derek. We have now assigned every regular guest to a floor.

The only floor with at least three regular guests is the 1st floor, so 1A, 1B, and 1C are occupied by regular guests (clue 2). Zach, therefore, can't be above any of those rooms and is in 2D or 2E (clue 3). But if Zach were in 2E, three sailing club members would occupy E rooms, which would contradict clue 6, since we know 1A is occupied by a regular guest. So Zach is in 2D, and sailing club members occupy 1D, 2B, and 3D. Phoebe is the only sailing club member on the 1st floor, so she's in 1D and Siobhan is in 3D (clue 9).

With 1D occupied, Olivia and Taylor can only be in 1C and 1E in some order (clue 5), which leaves Greg and Emma in 1A and 1B in some order, with Rory and Logan in the corresponding rooms on the 3rd floor (clues 8 and 10). But if Logan is in 3A and Rory in 3B, it's impossible to fulfill clue 7, so Rory is in 3A, Logan is in 3B (which puts James in 3C per clue 7), Greg is in 1A, and Emma is in 1B. Every regular guest on the 3rd floor is now accounted for, so Derek must be directly below one of them (clue 4). We already know 2B is occupied by the sailing club member who is across from Zach, so Derek is in 2C and Abby is in 2E.

We already know that Olivia and Taylor are in rooms 1C and 1E in some order. Maria and Taylor have rooms with the same letter (clue 11), so Taylor can't be in 1C, since 2C and 3C are occupied by Derek and James respectively. Taylor is therefore in 1E (placing Olivia in 1C), and Maria is in the only unoccupied E room, 3E. By elimination, Brent is the sailing club member in 2B, and 2A is empty.

Puzzle 4.4: Sailing the Seven Seas

Zach and Emma sailed the *Sea Horse* and finished first.
Rory and Taylor sailed the *Sea Robin* and finished second.
Siobhan and Logan sailed the *Sea Star* and finished third.
Brent and Abby sailed the *Sea Lion* and finished fourth.
Derek and Olivia sailed the *Sea Urchin* and finished fifth.
Maria and Greg sailed the *Sea Otter* and finished sixth.
Phoebe and James sailed the *Sea Anemone* and finished seventh.

The pairings in clues 1, 2, and 3 mean that the other four people or boats not mentioned in each clue are similarly paired among themselves in some combination.

Since the *Sea Anemone* is not Brent's boat (clue 5), it must be the boat of Derek, Phoebe, or Siobhan (clue 2); but since neither Derek nor Siobhan could have been paired with any guest who could have been aboard the *Sea Anemone* (clues 1 and 3), Phoebe was on the *Sea Anemone* and was not paired with Abby.

Abby was not on the *Sea Horse* (clue 6), which must therefore have been Zach's boat, since none of the guests possibly paired with Maria and Rory were on the *Sea Horse*.

Siobhan was not on the *Sea Urchin* (clue 7). Since Brent finished ahead of at least three boats (clue 5) and the *Sea Urchin* finished behind at least four boats (clue 7), Brent also cannot have been on the *Sea Urchin*. By elimination, Derek was on the *Sea Urchin* and so could not have been paired with Emma (clue 7), nor with Logan (clue 4). Therefore, Derek was paired with Olivia. Emma wasn't paired with Siobhan (clue 7), so by elimination, Emma was paired with Zach on the *Sea Horse* and Logan was paired with Siobhan.

Since Logan was not on the *Sea Lion* (clue 4), Siobhan was not either, and they were together on the *Sea Star*. By elimination, Brent was on the *Sea Lion* and could have been paired only with Abby, since the other guests he could have been paired with were not on the *Sea Lion*.

Since Abby did not finish in the top three (clue 6) and Brent did not finish in the bottom three (clue 5), they came in fourth, the *Sea Anemone* came in seventh (clue 5), and the *Sea Horse* came in first (clue 6), with Emma and Zach aboard. Per clue 7, Siobhan was third (with Logan on the *Sea Star*), two places behind Emma, and the *Sea Urchin* (with Derek and Olivia) fifth.

Since Rory finished ahead of the *Sea Otter* (clue 8), by elimination Rory was aboard the *Sea Robin* and finished second and Maria was aboard the *Sea Otter* and finished sixth. Taylor,

having finished ahead of Maria (clue 9), wasn't paired with Phoebe (who finished seventh), so was paired with Rory and came in second. Since Olivia came in fifth and Abby came in fourth, clue 10 indicates that Greg came in sixth and was paired with Maria on the *Sea Otter*. By elimination, James was on the *Sea Anemone* with Phoebe and finished seventh.

Weekend 5

Puzzle 5.1: Secret Passages

The guests confer at length, and eventually come up with the correct solution:

Abby will end up in staff room S3.
Emma will end up in staff room S5.
Greg will end up in guest room 2D.
James will end up in the private study.
Logan will end up in the dining room.
Olivia will end up in staff room S7.
Taylor will end up in the art studio.

There are only two ways in or out of the guest wing: the first-floor hallway and the crawlspace at the end of the wing. Since the guest wing contains three guests and only one burr puzzle, one guest must exit via the hallway and the other via the crawlspace. To avoid crossing paths, Emma must use the crawlspace and take it all the way down to the tunnel to basement 2, Greg must end up in guest room 2D, and Abby must leave the wing via the first-floor hallway after going down the stairs.

The staff wing has only three access points: the first-floor hallway, the second-floor hallway, and the crawlspace on the side. Since the wing contains three burr puzzles, all three routes must be used. The crawlspace cannot be accessed or exited via the storage room on the first floor without blocking that hallway for another guest, and so it must be exited via the second-floor closet of staff room S5. This connects to basement 2, and so it must be Emma who goes up the crawlspace and ends up in S5.

The third floor, excluding the guest wing, has two ways in or out: the stairway to the second floor hallway and the crawlspace. To avoid crossing paths in the hallway, James must use the stairs and Logan the crawlspace. To avoid crossing James's path at the foot of the stairs that connect the second and third floors, Taylor must go from the small game room to the landing that leads to the foyer or to the other second-floor hall. James must go the other way and end up in the private study, since going past the study would block anyone else's access to it.

The burr puzzles in S3 and S7 must be accessed by guests using the first-floor hallway (plus the stairs) and the second-floor hallway, respectively. Since Olivia cannot leave the sitting room via the crawlspace, which is being used by Logan, she must proceed up the hallway between the private study and staff lounge. Her paths to the left will be blocked by Taylor and James, and so her destination must be S7.

Taylor must proceed to the foyer, art gallery, and art studio. (Going anywhere but the art studio from the foyer would prevent anyone else from reaching the art studio.) Logan must take the crawlspace down to the basement level, accessing basement 1 through the storage area and going up the stairs to the hallway. Since the foyer is visited by Taylor, Logan must go from there to the kitchen, which leaves no way for Abby to reach the dining room, so Logan continues on through the pantry to the dining room. Abby will proceed along the hallway around the kitchen to the staff wing, go up the stairs, and end up in S3.

Puzzle 5.2: Name Games

Abby wrote quiz 7, Emma wrote quiz 6, Greg wrote quiz 4, James wrote quiz 2, Logan wrote quiz 3, Olivia wrote quiz 1, and Taylor wrote quiz 5.

Abby had 40 solving points and 6 quiz-writing points for a total score of 46.

Emma had 21 solving points and 8 quiz-writing points for a total score of 29.

Greg had 13 solving points and 0 quiz-writing points for a total score of 13.

James had 18 solving points and 4 quiz-writing points for a total score of 22.

Logan had 14 solving points and 2 quiz-writing points for a total score of 16.

Olivia had 23 solving points and 2 quiz-writing points for a total score of 25.

Taylor had 38 solving points and 10 quiz-writing points for a total score of 48.

From clue 1, quizzes 1, 2, 5, and 7 were written by Abby, James, Olivia, and Taylor, in some combination.

Since the number of guests scoring 0 on each quiz was different for every quiz except 1 and 3 (which had one 0 score each, per clue 2), and since each quiz was taken by the six guests who did not write it, there must have been totals of 0, 2, 3, 4, and 5 0's for the other five quizzes. There were at least 16 scores of 0 (clue 3), but there cannot have been more than that, since there were 21 7's (clue 3) and five other scores (clues 4 and 5) among the 42 quizzes taken, and $16 + 21 + 5 = 42$, so that accounts for all the scores. All eight of Abby and Taylor's scores for quizzes 1, 2, 3, and 4 were the same (clue 12), so they must have been all 0's or all 7's They can't have been all 0's, since quiz 1 and quiz 3 each had only one 0 score, so Abby and Taylor each scored 7 on quizzes 1 through 4, which means neither of them wrote any of those quizzes. Abby scored 5 on quiz 5 (clue 5), so she didn't write that quiz either, and by elimination she wrote quiz 7. By further elimination, Taylor wrote quiz 5.

For Olivia's score to be half of James's on quiz 3 (clue 6), she either scored 2 or 3 while he scored 4 or 6. Since Greg's solving score was 1 point less than Logan's (clue 8), and Logan's solving points were a multiple of 7 (clues 3, 4, and 5), Greg must have scored 6 on one quiz. Therefore, James scored 4 and Olivia 2 on quiz 3. Greg scored 0 on quizzes 3 and 7 (clue 13), so he scored 6 on quiz 2 (clue 4). One of the four scores in clue 4 was scored on quiz 7. It wasn't scored by Abby (who wrote quiz 7), Emma or Logan (per clue 4), or Greg, James, or Olivia (who account for the three other scores in clue 4), so Taylor scored 3 on quiz 7.

How could Abby have come in second instead of first by virtue of scoring 5 points on quiz 5 instead of skipping it (clue 5)? The only possibility is that no one else scored any points on that quiz, and a 0 score by her would have meant 0 quiz-writing points for Taylor, who wrote that quiz. Instead, Taylor earned 10 for five 0's. So everyone else who took quiz 5 scored 0. From clue 11, James, Logan, and Olivia also scored 0 on quiz 6, so none of them wrote quiz 6. Since Greg also scored 0 on quiz 6 (clue 7), Emma must have written quiz 6. Quiz 6 has four 0 scores and can't have more, since quiz 5 is the test with five 0 scores, so Abby and Taylor each scored 7 on quiz 6. Quiz 1 had one 0 and no other scores but 7, and so it had five 7's. Quiz 3 had three 7's.

Based on quizzes whose authors are now known, and on eliminations already made, quizzes 1 and 2 were written by James and Olivia in some order, and quizzes 3 and 4 were written by Greg and Logan in some order. Greg scored 0 on quiz 3, so he didn't write it, which means Logan did, and Greg wrote quiz 4. Since Greg had the same number of 0's as the number of guests who scored 0 on quiz 6 (which was 4), and had 0's on quizzes 3, 5, 6, and 7, he must have scored 7 on quiz 1.

From clue 14, quiz 7 had three 0's, quiz 2 had two, and quiz 4 had none, and so quiz 4 had six 7s. Since Logan wrote quiz 3, Emma had the third 7 score on it.

From clue 10, James wrote quiz 2 (which had two 0 scores) and Olivia wrote quiz 1 (which had one 0 score). For Olivia to have finished ahead of James in solving points despite his 7 on quiz 7 (clue 9), she must have had 7's on quizzes 2 and 7 while James had the only 0 on quiz 1.

Since quiz 7 had three 0's, Emma and Logan both had 0's on that quiz. They also both scored 7's on quiz 1 and 0's on quiz 2.

Had Abby not tried quiz 5, she would have had 5 fewer solving points but Taylor would have had 10 fewer quiz-writing points, and she would have won the competition by 3 points instead of losing by 2.

Quiz answers and explanations

Quiz 1:
Names appear in consecutive letters within each sentence. (#1: Olivia, in TripOLI VIA; #2: Abby, in lAB BY; #3: Taylor, in sTAY LORdship; #4: Emma, in seEM MAd; #5: James, in JAM EScarole; #6: Logan, in bLOG ANd; #7: Greg, in biG REGret.)

Quiz 2:
The numbers are the alphabetical positions of the first and last letters in each name, run together. E.g., Emma = E, A = 5,1 = 51. (#1: Emma; #2: Greg; #3: Abby; #4: Olivia; #5: James; #6: Logan; #7: Taylor.)

Quiz 3:
The letters in the name, added to the clue words in order, form new words; in some cases the letters in the name are all placed in front of the words in the clue, in other cases all are placed at the end. (#1: James, letters added to front; #2: Logan, letters added to front; #3: Emma, letters added to front; #4: Abby, letters added to end; #5: Olivia, letters added to front; #6: Taylor, letters added to end; #7: Greg, letters added to end.)

Quiz 4:
The letters are replaced by other letters of the alphabet, with A and Z standing for one another, B and Y standing for one another, etc. (#1: Taylor; #2: Olivia; #3: Logan; #4: James; #5: Greg; #6: Emma; #7: Abby.)

Quiz 5:
Names are encrypted using the same method used to encrypt the message in the Memorable Mosaic. To decode, write each digit as a two-digit number in base 3, and put all those two-digit numbers on separate lines, in order. Then read down the columns three digits at a time and convert those three-digit base 3 numbers to letters, with 001 = A, 002 = B, 010 = C, etc., through 222 = Z. (For example, the six digits of #1 translate to 00, 00, 12, 02, 02, and 21 in base 3; if you write those six numbers on different lines and read

down each column, you get 001, 002, 002, 221, which translates to A, B, B, and Y in base 3. The nine digits of #4 translate to 10, 01, 12, 02, 00, 11, 10, 10, and 10, which, when reading down the columns, become 101, 001, 111, 012, 201, 000, which translates to J, A, M, E, S, and a blank character.) Abby guessed that the shorter numbers were the shorter names and guessed that all the answers were in alphabetical order, but that meant that she got two wrong. (#1: Abby; #2: Greg; #3: Emma; #4: James; #5: Logan; #6: Olivia; #7: Taylor.)

Quiz 6:
Names are composed of the letters of the alphabet not found in each word list. (#1: Logan; #2: Greg; #3: James; #4: Olivia; #5: Emma; #6: Abby; #7: Taylor.)

Quiz 7:
Names appear as initial letters of successive words within each sentence. (#1: James, Jokes A Magician Ever Says; #2: Greg, Get Ready Everyone Get; #3: Taylor, Taken At Yesterday's Lavish Office Reunion; #4: Logan, Land Of Grapes And Nuts; #5: Abby, A Bad Break Yesterday; #6: Olivia, Our Logo Is Very Important As; #7, Emma, Every Monster Movie And.)

Puzzle 5.3: Snark Hunting

Choosing envelopes 1, 2, 3, 9, and 10 or envelopes 4, 5, 6, 7, and 8 will give you a complete set of the letters S, N, A, R, and K on both blue and green cards.

Envelope 1 contains S (green) and N (blue).
Envelope 2 contains A (green) and R (blue).
Envelope 3 contains N (green) and K (blue).
Envelope 4 contains S (green) and A (blue).
Envelope 5 contains R (green) and K (blue).
Envelope 6 contains N (blue) and A (green).
Envelope 7 contains S (blue) and K (green).
Envelope 8 contains N (green) and R (blue).
Envelope 9 contains A (blue) and K (green).
Envelope 10 contains S (blue) and R (green).

(Once you know what each envelope contains, you can see that, to form a solution, no set of five envelopes can contain two identical cards; so, for example, a solution including envelope 1 cannot include envelope 4 or 6, each of which has a card matching a card in envelope 1. Then you can similarly see that a solution with envelope 4 cannot include envelope 9, and a solution with envelope 6 cannot include envelope 2. Continuing in this way, the two combinations that work are quickly found.)

From clues 4 and 5, envelope 3 must contain a K; otherwise, envelope 3 would have to contain either the same two letters as envelope 1 in contradiction of clue 3, or one of the two letters in envelope 2 in contradiction of clue 4. More broadly, each letter must appear at least once within each set of three consecutively numbered envelopes to avoid a contradiction with clue 3 or 4. Since envelope 3 contains a K, envelope 4 does not.

Similarly, from clue 6, envelopes 6 and 9 contain A's and envelopes 5 and 10 do not. The four A's must be in envelopes 6, 9, and two of the envelopes 1 through 4. From clue 7, envelope 6 does not contain a K, and so the K cards must be in envelopes 3, 5, and two of the envelopes from 7 through 10. The two lowest-numbered K envelopes are 3 and 5, which add up to 8, and these are on blue

cards (clue 8). The green A cards must be in two envelopes adding up to 8, which can only be 2 and 6. The A's on blue cards must be in envelopes 4 and 9.

Since no two envelopes contain the same combination of letters, every possible combination of letters appears in some envelope. (There are exactly 10 different ways of choosing two items from a set of five.) The combination of A and K can only be in envelope 9, since A and K do not appear together in envelopes 1 through 6 and A does not appear in envelopes 7, 8, or 10. K therefore appears on green cards in envelopes 7 and 9.

S, N, and R must appear together in the three combinations of S-N, N-R, and S-R in envelopes 1, 8, and 10 in some order, since the other envelopes contain A and/or K. From clues 4 and 5, envelopes 1 and 2 together contain one N and one R. If envelope 10 contained an N, the lowest possible sum of envelopes containing N (remembering that each letter must appear at least once within each set of three consecutively numbered envelopes) would be $1 + 4 + 7 + 10 = 22$, and the highest possible total for R would be $2 + 5 + 8 + 10 = 25$, not enough to account for the difference of 7 in clue 9. And so, envelope 10 does not include an N, and must contain an S and an R. Since envelope 9 contains an A and a K, envelope 8 must contain an N, and it is on a green card (clue 10).

If envelope 8 does not also contain an R, the N-R combination must be in envelope 1. But in that case, N's envelope number total would be at least $1 + 3 + 5 + 8 = 17$, whereas R's total would be at most $1 + 4 + 7 + 10 = 22$, not enough to account for the difference of 7. So envelope 8 must contain an R, and it is on a blue card since envelope 8's N card is green. The other envelopes containing R must be 2 and 5, since otherwise more than two consecutive envelopes would lack an R. The R in envelope 2 is on a blue card (since the A card in that envelope is green), the R in envelope 5 is on a green card (since the K card in that envelope is blue), and by elimination the R in envelope 10 is on a green card, which means the S in envelope 10 is on a blue card. Having identified the letters in envelopes 8 and 10, by elimination the letters in envelope 1 are S and N.

An N must appear within three envelopes of the N in envelope 8, and since envelope 5 contains R and K, envelope 6 must contain that N, which is on a blue card (since A's card there is green). For the sum of the N envelopes to be 7 less than that of the R envelopes, envelope 3 contains an N, on a green card (since the K card there is blue). By elimination, the N in envelope 1 is on a blue card, and the S in that envelope is on a green card.

The envelopes without two letters accounted for are 4 and 7, and so those each contain an S, on a green card in envelope 4 and a blue card in envelope 7.

Weekend 6

Puzzle 6.1: Regatta

The order of finish in each race and each sailor's total points are shown in the grid at the top of the next page. James won the guest trophy and Rory won the sailing club trophy.

	Race 1	Race 2	Race 3	Race 4	Race 5	Race 6	Race 7	total points
regular summer guests								
Abby	7	5	6	4	1	4	1	28
Emma	3	3	3	1	2	2	5	19
Greg	6	4	2	3	3	6	6	30
James	2	1	1	2	5	3	4	18
Logan	4	6	5	7	6	7	7	42
Olivia	5	2	7	6	7	5	3	35
Taylor	1	7	4	5	4	1	2	24
sailing club members								
Brent	7	7	7	7	5	6	5	44
Derek	3	5	4	6	6	3	6	33
Maria	6	3	6	5	7	7	4	38
Phoebe	2	4	3	4	4	5	7	29
Rory	4	1	2	1	1	1	3	13
Siobhan	5	6	1	3	2	4	2	23
Zach	1	2	5	2	3	2	1	16

The sailing club member who finished last four times in a row (clue 1) must have finished last in race 4. From the pairings, the club member who finished last in race 4 cannot be Rory, Siobhan, or Zach, since they were paired with Emma, Greg, and James, none of whom ever finished last (clue 2). Nor can it be Phoebe, who only finished last once.

Olivia and Taylor were paired with Derek and Maria in race 4. Since neither finished last (clue 3), the club member who finished last four times in a row must be Brent. Since Logan was paired with Brent in race 4 and thus finished last in that race, Taylor finished fifth and Olivia sixth (as did Maria and Derek, respectively). Since Brent was paired with James, Greg, and Emma in the final three races, none of whom ever finished last, the first three races were the other ones in which Brent finished last, as did his paired guests Abby, Taylor, and Olivia.

From the list of club members paired with Logan, Greg, and Olivia (none of whom, from clues 5 and 15, ever finished first), the winner of races 4, 5, and 6 had to be Rory, along with partners Emma, Abby, and Taylor (clue 4).

Race 6 must be one of the two consecutive races in which a club member finished last (clue 1). It cannot have been lost by Derek or Zach, who were paired with James and Emma (neither of whom ever finished last), or by Brent or Phoebe (clue 1), nor by Siobhan (clue 7), and so it was Maria who finished last in race 6, along with her partner Logan. Since Maria was paired with James (who never came in last) in race 7, the other race she lost must have been race 5, when she was paired with Olivia, which means that Phoebe (and Logan) lost race 7.

From clues 8 and 15, Olivia, James, and Greg finished third, fourth, and sixth, respectively, in race 7, as did their partners Rory, Maria, and Derek. Then from clue 14, Taylor and Emma finished second and fifth, respectively, in race 7, as did their partners Siobhan and Brent, so the winners were Abby and Zach. Zach therefore finished second in race 6 with Emma and third in race 5 with Greg (clue 9).

Olivia was second in race 2 and Greg was second in race 3 (clue 15), as were their partners Zach and Rory. From clue 10, race 1 must be the other race won by Taylor, and so Olivia was fifth and Greg sixth in that race, their partners Zach, Siobhan, and Maria also finished first, fifth, and sixth, respectively. Also per clue 15,

Olivia and Greg finished fifth and six in race 6 as well, as did their partners Phoebe and Brent. James won twice (clue 6), and those wins can only have been in the second and third races, in which he was partnered with Rory and Siobhan.

The only guests who could have finished third in three consecutive races and ended up with as few as 19 points (clue 13) are Emma and James; for if Abby did it, she would end up with at least $7 + 3 + 3 + 3 + 1 + 3 + 1 = 21$ points. But since Greg finished third in race 5, there is no three-race stretch in which James could have finished third three times. Therefore, only Emma can have finished third three times in a row, and she must have done so in the first three races, along with her partners Derek, Maria, and Phoebe. Maria was sixth in race 3 (clue 12), with her partner Abby.

Clue 11 places James third and Abby fourth in race 6, along with their partners Derek and Siobhan.

In races 2, 4, and 5, Siobhan must have finished second, third, and sixth in some order (clue 7). Race 2 must be her sixth place finish (since Zach and Maria finished second and third in that race), and race 4 her third place finish (since Zach finished third in race 5); by elimination she finished second in race 5. Likewise, Logan finished sixth in race 2, Greg finished third in race 4, and Emma finished second in race 5. With only Abby and James unaccounted for among the guests in race 4, James must be second and Abby fourth (clue 11), along with their partners Zach and Phoebe.

Emma's point total after race 6 was 14. The only other guest with a low enough score to be tied with her at that point (per clue 16) is James, and therefore his point total in races 1 and 5 must add up to 7. That means he must have finished second in race 1 and fifth in race 5, as did his partners Phoebe and Brent. By elimination, Logan and Rory were fourth in race 1.

Rory's point total was 13, lower than anyone else's possible total, so Rory was the winning club member. Second place can only have gone to Zach, so Zach's point total must have been 16 (clue 17), and therefore he and Logan were fifth in race 3, and by elimination Derek and Taylor finished fourth. The totals 13 and 16 add up to 29, which can only have been Phoebe's total, and only if she finished fourth in both race 2 and race 5 (clue 17), along with her partners Greg and Taylor.

By elimination, Derek and Abby finished fifth in race 2, and Derek and Logan finished sixth in race 5.

Puzzle 6.2: Murder in the Wine Cellar

Olivia is the killer. Of the club members who were present at the Montauk meeting, which is when the coin theft occurred, she is the only one without an alibi for the hour in which the murder took place.

The first meeting, in Fort Lauderdale, was attended by Emma, James, Logan, and Olivia.

The second meeting, in Savannah, was attended by Abby, Grant, Greg, and James.

The third meeting, in Atlantic City, was attended by Abby, Emma, Logan, Olivia, and Taylor.

The fourth meeting, in Montauk, was attended by Emma, Grant, Greg, Olivia, and Taylor.

The fifth meeting, in Williamsburg, was attended by Abby, Greg, Logan, and Olivia.

The sixth meeting, in Newport, was attended by Emma, Grant, Greg, James, and Taylor.

The seventh meeting, in Myrtle Beach, was attended by Abby, James, Logan, and Taylor.

Gordon's statement indicates that each club member attended exactly four meetings, except that Grant only attended three. Greg's and Logan's statements identify four locations where Greg attended meetings and three locations where Grant attended, which means that Greg did not attend the meetings in Atlantic City, Fort Lauderdale, or Myrtle Beach, and the only meetings Grant attended were in Montauk, Newport, and Savannah. Since Emma's and Olivia's statements indicate that they did not attend the Myrtle Beach meeting either, the other four club members— Abby, James, Logan, and Taylor—must all have attended Myrtle Beach, as required by Sandy's statement. From Abby's and Logan's statements, the three meetings Abby attended besides Myrtle Beach were in Atlantic City, Savannah, and Williamsburg.

Per Abby's statement, the two meetings she attended besides Atlantic City and Savannah were the fifth and seventh meetings, so Myrtle Beach and Williamsburg were fifth and seventh in some order. Per James's statement, he was at the second, sixth, and seventh meetings, and Abby was also at the second meeting. Abby was not at the sixth meeting (since James was) and James was not at the fifth meeting (since Abby was). Since James was at Myrtle Beach but wasn't at the fifth meeting, Myrtle Beach was the seventh location and Williamsburg was the fifth.

Taylor was at the third, fourth, and sixth meetings (per Taylor's statement), so those three plus the seventh meeting in Myrtle Beach, which Taylor attended, account for all of Taylor's meetings. Taylor's two consecutive meetings in Atlantic City and Montauk couldn't have been the sixth and seventh (since the seventh was in Myrtle Beach), so they were third and fourth in some order. Per Sandy's statement, Montauk wasn't the third meeting, so it was fourth and Atlantic City was third. Since Abby attended the third meeting in Atlantic City, James did not (per his statement). With the second, fifth, and seventh meetings, that accounts for all of Abby's meetings, so by elimination, Savannah was second. Per James's statement, Fort Lauderdale wasn't the sixth meeting, so it was first, and by elimination Newport was sixth. Per Sandy's statement, the three meetings attended by five people were the third (in Atlantic City), the fourth (in Montauk), and the sixth (in Newport); the rest were attended by four people.

We know the locations that Grant and Greg attended, so we know they both attended the second, fourth, and sixth meetings, and Greg additionally attended the fifth meeting. Per Logan's statement, Abby, Greg, Logan, and Olivia account for everyone attending the fifth meeting in Williamsburg. James attended the first meeting in Fort Lauderdale (per his statement), and from previous deductions we know his remaining meetings were in Savannah, Newport, and Myrtle Beach. Per Olivia, Emma and Olivia both attended the first meeting in Fort Lauderdale, the third in Atlantic City, and the fourth in Montauk. Emma also attended the sixth in Newport (per Taylor), which accounts for her four meetings, and we already know Olivia attended the fifth in Williamsburg, so she is also fully accounted for. From previous deductions, we know Taylor attended meetings in Atlantic City, Montauk, Myrtle Beach, and Newport. We also already know Logan attended Myrtle Beach and Williamsburg; based on the number of people who attended each meeting, his remaining meetings were the first in Fort Lauderdale and the third in Atlantic City.

Since Grant was not at the third or fifth meetings, it follows from Charlotte's clue that the coin theft must have occurred at the fourth meeting. Abby, James, and Logan did not attend the fourth meeting and are therefore innocent. When James and Logan said they were in their rooms from 5 to 6 P.M., they were telling the truth. Emma has alibis for that hour from Sandy and Abby. Since Olivia did not attend the sixth club meeting, that leaves Greg

and Taylor as the two that Lyle stated were in the big game room between 5 and 6 P.M., which gives them an alibi. (In case it isn't clear why Greg's statement is true, note that the big game room is on the second floor, per the map on page 33.) Since everyone else has an alibi, Olivia must be the guilty one, and lied about her whereabouts.

Puzzle 6.3: Speed Darts

First round
Taylor shot 11, double 11, and triple 11 for a score of 66.
Nolan shot 5, 17, and triple 17 for a score of 73.
Abby shot double 3, triple 3, and triple 20 for a score of 75.
Olivia shot 13, double 13, and triple 13 for a score of 78.
James shot 4, double 4, and 16, for a score of 28.
Logan shot 1, double 1, and triple 19 for a score of 60.
Greg shot 7, 18, and double 18 for a score of 61.
Emma shot 3, 20, and double 20 for a score of 63.

Second round
Taylor shot triple 4, double 16, and triple 16 for a score of 92.
Nolan shot double 7, triple 7, and triple 18 for a score of 89.
Abby shot 15, triple 9, and triple 15 for a score of 87.
Olivia shot 19, 25, and double 19 for a score of 82.

Third round
Taylor shot double 5, double 17, and 50 for a score of 94.
Nolan shot double 14, triple 10, and triple 14 for a score of 100.

The first-round scores of Olivia and Taylor must each be divisible by 6, since they each shot a single, double, and triple of the same number (clue 4), so two of the scores 60, 66, and 78 must be theirs. But since they both advanced to the second round (per clues 6 and 8), neither of them scored 60, which was one of the four lowest scores in the first round. Divided by 6, the totals of 66 and 78 indicate they used the 11 and 13 wedges of the dartboard (scoring single, double, and triple of each number). Per clue 12, Olivia's second-highest scoring dart in this round was higher than Taylor's, so Olivia scored 78 and Taylor scored 66.

Since Abby and Emma used all six possible numbers along one line (clues 1 and 5), they hit the single, double, and triple values of two different numbers, and so the sum of their scores must be divisible by six. (Since no two darts ever scored the same, neither Abby nor Emma could have thrown a bullseye, because Olivia and Taylor did in later rounds.) Only three first-round scores are divisible by six, and two of them belonged to Olivia and Taylor; therefore Abby and Emma must have scores that, when divided by 6, have remainders that add up to six. The only possibilities are 63 and 75, each of which has a remainder of 3 when divided by 6. The sum of the two scores is 138, or 6 × 23. The only pair of numbers across from one another on the dartboard that add up to 23 are 20 and 3. Abby must have the higher score, since she advanced to the second round (per clue 10), so Emma scored 63 with shots of 3, 20, and double 20, and Abby scored 75 with shots of double 3, triple 3, and triple 20.

When divided by 6, the other first-round scores have remainders of 1 (for 61 and 73) and 4 (for 28). When divided by 6, the second-round scores have remainders of 4 (for 82), 5 (for 89), 3 (for 87), and 2 (for 92). James in the first round and Taylor in the second-round together hit all six possible values in two wedges lying on the same line (clue 6), so their scores, when divided by 6, must have combined remainders adding up to 6. The same is true of Greg's first-round score and Nolan's second-round score (clue 7). One pair of scores with remainders, when divided by 6, that add up to 6 is 28 and 92, and the other is 89 and either 61 or 73. But 89 and 73 add up to 162, which is 6×27, and no two numbers that are directly across from one another on the dartboard add up to 27. Therefore, the scores of 61 and 89 lie along the same line; and since their total is 150, which equals 6×25, they must all fall on the line connecting the 7 and 18 wedges of the dartboard, the only pair of opposite numbers adding up to 25. As for the scores of 28 and 92, they add up to 120, which equals 6×20, and so were all made in the 4 and 16 wedges of the dartboard. (It can't be the 1 and 19 wedges because then one dart would have scored 2 points, but from clue 11 Logan had a 2-point dart, and no two darts had the same score, per clue 1.) James and Greg, therefore, had first-round scores of 28 and 61, in some combination, and Nolan and Taylor had second-round scores of 89 and 92, in some combination. By elimination Abby and Olivia had second-round scores of 82 and 87, in some combination.

The score of 28 was formed by 4, double 4, and 16, and the 92 by triple 4, double 16, and triple 16. The score of 61 was made by 7, 18, and double 18, and the score of 89 by double 7, triple 7, and triple 18. We know that James and Greg scored 28 and 61 in the first round in some combination. The second-highest scoring darts for those scores scored 8 and 18, respectively. Per clue 12, Greg's second-best dart scored higher than James's, so Greg scored 61 and James scored 28 (which means Nolan scored 89 and Taylor scored 92 in the second round).

By elimination, Logan and Nolan scored 60 and 73 in some order, but since Nolan advanced to the second round (clue 7), Logan scored 60 and Nolan scored 73. One of Logan's darts scored 2 (clue 11). If that dart was a single 2, it would not be possible to score 58 with two more darts on the 2–12 line, so the 2 must be a double 1 from the 1–19 line, and Logan scored 60 with 1, double 1, and triple 19. Olivia used the same line in the second round (clue 8), with possible scores of 82 and 87. Since Olivia threw a 25-point dart, Olivia's other darts scored 57 or 62. Of the three unused scores in that line (3, 19, and 38), the only pair that works is $19 + 38 = 57$, so Olivia scored 82 with 19, 25, and double 19, and by elimination Abby scored 87 in the second round.

Abby's score of 87 wasn't on the 6–11 or 8–13 lines (each already used by Olivia and Taylor in the first round and thus not used again, per clue 10), so we can ignore those, as well as the 2–12 and 10–14 lines, since an odd-numbered score is impossible on a line with no odd numbers. Her score is impossible to make on the 5–17 line (17×6 is too high and 5×6 is too low; the only multiple of 17 lower than 6 that leaves a remainder from 87 that's a multiple of 5 is 17 itself, and it's obviously impossible to score 70 with two darts in the 5 wedge), so her scores were on the 9–15 line, and can only have been 15, triple 9, and triple 15. No one else used that line (clue 10).

Nolan's first-round score of 73 was on the same line as Taylor's third-round score (clue 9). Taylor scored either 94 or 100 in that round, which would be 44 or 50 if Taylor's 50-point dart is excluded. Their scores were not on the 2–12 or 10–14 lines, odd-numbered scores being impossible on lines with no odd numbers, so they used the 5–17 line. One of Abby's darts scored 15, so the triple 5 can't have been scored on this line (clue 1), which leaves a total of 117 for the five darts that didn't hit the bullseye. Since $73 + 44 = 117$, Taylor scored 94. Nolan's 73 was scored with 5, 17, and triple 17, and Taylor scored 94 with double 5, double 17, and the bullseye.

Nolan in the third round scored 100 in one of the two remaining unused lines. It's impossible to score that much in the 2–12 line, so his darts landed in the 10–14 line, scoring 100 with double 14, triple 10, and triple 14.

For the record, the only possible number that no one threw was 24 (double 12 or triple 8).

Weekend 7

Puzzle 7.1: Web of Lies

The killers are Emma, James, and Logan, all of whose statements are false.

Since there are at most three killers (Evelyn's statement), there cannot be more than three guests who make false statements (Charlotte's statement).

Because their statements contradict, we know that either Abby or James is lying, but not both, and that Emma or Greg is lying, but not both. So there are at least two liars.

If Logan's statement is true, then whichever of Abby and Greg lied contradicts Taylor, and Taylor's statement is false; but since either Abby or Greg also told the truth, we know that of the statements of Emma and James, one is true and the other is false. This is inconsistent with Olivia's statement, which means that if Logan is telling the truth, both Olivia and Taylor are lying, which makes a total of four killers.

Logan's statement is therefore false, so Logan is the third killer. To avoid there being more than three false statements, Taylor's statement must be true, which lets us quickly determine that the other false statements were spoken by Emma and James.

Puzzle 7.2: ESP Test

From left to right: square, plus sign, circle, star, wavy lines

Emma and James have no guesses in common, but between them four of their guesses are correct. Consider James's guesses in light of each possible correct pair of Emma's guesses.

If Emma's guesses of the first two cards are correct, James's are not, nor is James's fourth card guess; but James's third and fifth card guesses could be, giving a possible answer of plus sign, circle, wavy lines, square, star. But in that case, Logan would have had two correct guesses, not one, so that is not the correct sequence of cards.

If Emma's first and third card guesses are correct, only James's fourth and fifth card guesses can be, giving a possible answer of plus sign, wavy lines, square, circle, star. But in that case as well, Logan would have had two correct guesses, not one, so that is not the correct sequence of cards.

If Emma guessed the first and fourth or first and fifth cards correctly, James could not have had more than one correct guess, which contradicts Gordon's statement. The same is true if Emma guessed the second and third cards correctly, and so she did not.

If Emma guessed the second and fourth cards correctly, James could have correctly guessed the first and third, giving a possible answer of square, circle, wavy lines, star, and plus sign. But in that case Greg would have had no correct guesses, not one, so that is not the correct sequence of cards.

If Emma guessed the second and fifth or third and fourth cards correctly, James could not have had more than one correct guess, so those were not Emma's correct guesses.

If Emma guessed the third and fifth cards correctly, James could have correctly guessed the second and fourth, giving a possible answer of star, plus sign, square, circle, wavy lines. But in that case Greg would again have had no correct guesses, giving us another contradiction.

If Emma guessed the fourth and fifth cards correctly, James's guess of the first two cards could have been correct, giving a possible answer of square, plus sign, circle, star, wavy lines. That sequence is also consistent with Greg's and Logan's statements and is the answer.

Puzzle 7.3: Shell Game

As a shorthand, let the letters A, B, C, D, and E stand for clam shell, conch shell, cowrie shell, oyster shell, and scallop shell, respectively. The shells are initially arranged like this:
1. AAAAA
2. BBBBB
3. CCCCC
4. DDDDD
5. EEEEE

Allowable exchanges are:
AA for DDD
AB for CDE
AD for EE
BB for DD
BBB for CC
BC for ADE
BC for EE

One order of exchanges that works is:
BBB-CC (placemats 2 and 3)
BC-EE (placemats 3 and 5)
BB-DD (placemats 3 and 4)
AA-DDD (placemats 1 and 4)
AD-EE (placemats 1 and 5)
BC-ADE (placemats 1 and 2)
AB-CDE (placemats 3 and 4)

(Various steps can be slightly reordered; for instance, the last two steps can be done in either order, and the AA-DDD exchange can be moved anywhere earlier in the sequence.)

The two steps BC-ADE and AB-CDE involve movement of all five types of shells, so they will need to be the last two steps. By working backward from them, it is clear that after five turns, one placemat must already contain five different shells and the others contain the combinations AADDEE, BBCC, CCDDEE, and AABB, so that the final two exchanges will complete the solution. A placemat with BBCC can be achieved with the first exchange of BBB-CC between placemats 2 and 3. The two exchanges AD-EE and BC-EE must have taken place before the final two steps; to achieve the positions above, the two EE pairs must have moved to two different placemats from placemat 5, and so placemat 5 is the one that already has a complete ABCDE set before the last two exchanges.

After the BBB-CC exchange, placemat 2 must be left alone until the last two exchanges. The only exchange remaining before the final two that involves any C's is BC-EE, so that exchange must involve placemat 3, the only other placemat with C's. We can make that exchange now with placemat 5, after which placemat 2 has BBCCEE. From there, an exchange of BB-DD with placemat 4 will give placemat 2 CCDDEE, another one of our goal combinations, so we are now also done with placemat 3 until the last two exchanges.

After the BB-DD swap, placemat 4 has BBDDD, and only two exchanges remain before the final two: AA-DDD and AD-EE. No placemat has both A's and D's, so we can make the AA-DDD swap only between placemats 1 and 4, which leaves our target configuration AABB on placemat 4 and AAADDD on placemat 1,

after which we can make the AD-EE exchange between placemats 1 and 5, giving us AADDEE on placemat 1 and leaving us in position to make the final two exchanges.

Here are the sets of shells on each placemat after each trade:
AAAAA, BBCC, BBBCCC, DDDDD, EEEEE
AAAAA, BBCC, BBCCEE, DDDDD, BCEEE
AAAAA, BBCC, CCDDEE, BBDDD, BCEEE
AAADDD, BBCC, CCDDEE, AABB, BCEEE
AADDEE, BBCC, CCDDEE, AABB, ABCDE
ABCDE, ABCDE, CCDDEE, AABB, ABCDE
ABCDE, ABCDE, ABCDE, ABCDE, ABCDE

Puzzle 7.4: Truth Counts

1. Two. Any two of these statements can be true and the third false.

2. Two. James's and Olivia's statements can be true when the other two are false.

3. Zero; none of these statements can be true. If any statement is true, at least one statement must be false. Let's assume Abby's statement is false, bearing in mind our assumption that at least one statement is true. If Abby's statement is false, the next two statements (Emma's and Greg's) are either both true or both false. If they are both false, every other statement must also be false. (For instance, if Emma's statement is false, the following two statements must be both true or both false. Greg's is false, so James's is false as well. This reasoning continues throughout the sequence.) This contradicts our assumption that at least one statement is true. So, in this hypothetical, every false statement must be followed by two true statements. Furthermore, any two true statements must be followed by a false statement. (For instance, look at Emma and Greg's statements; Abby's statement is false so theirs are true. For Emma's statement to be true, either Greg's or James's must be false, but Greg's is true, so James's is false.) This repeating pattern of FTT can only be consistent with a sequence of statements that's divisible by three, but since there are seven statements here, this sequence will soon contradict itself. (In this case, we have: Abby F, Emma T, Greg T, James F, Logan T, Olivia T, Taylor F—and then we have a contradiction, because a true statement should follow, but Abby's is false.) Therefore it cannot be the case that any statements are true.

Weekend 8

Puzzle 8.1: Beach Volleyball

Cheryl and Nolan defeated Abby and James in the finals. In the semifinals, Cheryl and Nolan defeated Rory and Taylor, while Abby and James upset Siobhan and Zach.

In the double round-robin:
Siobhan and Zach, wearing black, finished first with a record of 7–3.
Cheryl and Nolan, wearing gold, finished second on tiebreak with a record of 6–4.
Rory and Taylor, wearing blue, finished third with a record of 6–4.
Abby and James, wearing white, finished fourth on tiebreak with a record of 5–5.
Emma and Logan, wearing red, finished fifth with a record of 5–5.
Greg and Olivia, wearing green, finished sixth with a record of 1–9.

The crosstable at the top of the next page shows the results of all the matches in the double round-robin.

	vs.1	vs.2	vs.3	vs.4	vs.5	vs.6	W–L
1st	✕	1–1	2–0	1–1	1–1	2–0	7–3
2nd	1–1	✕	1–1	1–1	1–1	2–0	6–4
3rd	0–2	1–1	✕	1–1	2–0	2–0	6–4
4th	1–1	1–1	1–1	✕	1–1	1–1	5–5
5th	1–1	1–1	0–2	1–1	✕	2–0	5–5
6th	0–2	0–2	0–2	1–1	0–2	✕	1–9

(row label: team won-lost records)

Since there were 30 games in the double round-robin, the won-lost records of all the teams must add up to 30–30. Since one team ended up 1–9 but is the only team with a worse record than 5–5 (clue 1), and since two pairs of teams tied with identical won-lost records (clue 2), the records of the teams must have been 7–3, 6–4, 6–4, 5–5, 5–5, and 1–9.

From clue 3, and the fact that the sixth-place team must have accounted for four of the six 2–0 matches, it is possible to complete the crosstable. (There must have been six 2–0 matches, because every match that wasn't one of the nine 1–1 matches ended 2–0.) The matches in which the third-place team lost 0–2 to the first-place team and beat the fifth-place team 2–0 were therefore the only 2–0 matches of all the matches among the teams from first to fifth, and all the rest were 1–1. For the fourth-place and fifth-place teams to end up tied at 5–5, the fourth-place team must have gone 1–1 against the sixth-place team (which was 0–2 against everyone else), and now every match's score is accounted for.

Based on the crosstable, whichever team finished in second place won its tiebreaker because it had a better record against the first-place team, and whichever team finished in fourth won its tiebreaker because it had a better record against the third-place team (the fourth- and fifth-place teams' records agains the top two teams were identical). Of the tied teams mentioned in clue 2, if the gold and blue teams finished in fourth and fifth, the black team finished third. That would leave only first and second place available for the white and red team (clue 5), placing Greg and Olivia in third. But per clue 2, the third-place team must be Emma and Logan, since they were the loser of the other tiebreaker, so this is a contradiction, and the gold and blue teams must have finished second and third respectively, with the black team in first. In the other tiebreaker, Abby and James finished fourth, beating Emma and Logan in fifth because of their better record against Rory and Taylor, who were the third-place blue team.

The colors of the top three teams are known, so the white and red teams can only have finished in fourth and fifth place respectively, with Greg and Olivia in sixth (clue 5). By elimination, the sixth-place team wore green. All the teams' placements are now accounted for except Cheryl-Nolan and Siobhan-Zach, who finished first and second in some combination. Since Cheryl and Nolan finished either two places better or worse than Abby and James in fourth place (clue 6), they finished second, and Siobhan and Zach finished first.

Since Siobhan and Zach defeated Rory and Taylor 2–0 in the double round-robin, these teams did not meet in the finals (clue 7), so at least one of these teams lost in the semifinals. If Siobhan and Zach won their semifinal game, then so did Cheryl and Nolan; but in that case, the upset (clue 4) would have to have been a win by Cheryl and Nolan over Siobhan and Zach in the finals, which contradicts clue 8. Therefore, Siobhan and Zach lost their semifinal game in an upset, and Cheryl and Nolan won both their semifinal and final games.

Puzzle 8.2: Barbecue

Abby drank fruit punch and had a veggie burger, baked potato, asparagus, balsamic vinaigrette, and chocolate chip ice cream.

Cheryl drank iced tea and had a hamburger, corn, asparagus, French dressing, and chocolate chip ice cream.

Emma drank lemonade and had a hamburger, corn, asparagus, ranch dressing, and peach ice cream.

Greg drank sarsaparilla and had ribs, corn, zucchini, balsamic vinaigrette, and chocolate chip ice cream.

James drank lemonade and had ribs, corn, asparagus, balsamic vinaigrette, and peach ice cream.

Logan drank iced tea and had a veggie burger, corn, zucchini, balsamic vinaigrette, and chocolate chip ice cream.

Nolan drank fruit punch and had chicken, baked potato, zucchini, French dressing, and pistachio ice cream.

Olivia drank sarsaparilla and had a hamburger, corn, asparagus, ranch dressing, and pistachio ice cream.

Rory drank lemonade and had salmon, baked potato, zucchini, French dressing, and peach ice cream.

Siobhan drank fruit punch and had salmon, corn, asparagus, French dressing, and chocolate chip ice cream.

Taylor drank iced tea and had a hamburger, corn, asparagus, ranch dressing, and pistachio ice cream.

Zach drank sarsaparilla and had salmon, corn, asparagus, blue cheese dressing, and chocolate chip ice cream.

From clues 1, 2, 3, and 5, four people had hamburgers, three had salmon, at least two had ribs, at least two had veggie burgers, and at least one had chicken. Since this accounts for all 12 main courses, exactly two had ribs, two had veggie burgers, and one had chicken, and only the people mentioned in clues 1 and 2 could have had chicken, ribs, or veggie burgers. Therefore, neither Olivia nor Taylor ordered ribs or veggie burgers, and only one person besides Rory and Siobhan ordered salmon (clue 3), and so for their main courses to match (clue 4), Olivia and Taylor both must have had hamburgers along with their pistachio ice cream.

From clue 12, Emma did not use blue cheese dressing and so did not have salmon (clue 3). By elimination, Zach had salmon and was the only one to have blue cheese dressing. Emma didn't have chicken, ribs, or a veggie burger either (since, as shown in the previous paragraph, only people mentioned in clues 1 or 2 did), so by elimination she had a hamburger.

Three people with hamburgers used ranch dressing (clue 5), so at least four people used balsamic vinaigrette (clue 11). Since no one who ate chicken, hamburgers, or salmon used balsamic vinaigrette (clues 5, 16, 17), the four who ate ribs and veggie burgers all did, and only those four (which means no more than three people had ranch). Four, then, had French: the person who had chicken, one person who had a hamburger, and two people who had salmon (which must be Rory and Siobhan, per clue 3).

One of the remaining two people who had French dressing is Abby, Cheryl, or Emma (clue 12), and since Logan did not have a hamburger (clue 2), he didn't have ranch dressing (since all three who had ranch dressing also had hamburgers, per clue 5). Therefore, for Greg and Logan's salad dressings to match (clue 14), they had to both have balsamic vinaigrette. This also means Greg did not have a hamburger.

From clues 8 and 16, since James had peach ice cream and Logan had balsamic vinaigrette, neither had chicken. By elimination, then, Nolan had chicken, used French dressing, and is the third person with pistachio ice cream (clue 16). Olivia and Taylor both had ranch dressing (clue 7).

The two who along with James had peach ice cream and the same drink (clue 8) cannot be Cheryl and Logan (since the other person who drank iced tea had pistachio ice cream, per clue 7) or Greg and Zach (two sarsaparilla drinkers who had chocolate chip ice cream, per clue 9) or clue 6's fruit punch drinkers Nolan and Siobhan (since Nolan had pistachio ice cream). Therefore, lemonade was the drink of James and the others who had peach ice cream. Since their ice cream flavors were not peach, Olivia and Taylor did not drink lemonade. Since they drank something other than lemonade, Cheryl, Logan, and Siobhan did not have peach ice cream and therefore had chocolate chip.

Since James had peach ice cream, he did not have a veggie burger (clue 13) and must have had ribs as well as balsamic vinaigrette (since all who ate ribs had balsamic vinaigrette).

From clues 8, 13, and 16, the peach ice cream eaters had a hamburger, ribs, and salmon (since three different main courses were had by those with peach ice cream, and everyone who had a veggie burger or chicken had another kind of ice cream). The only person who had salmon and did not have an ice cream flavor other than peach is Rory, who therefore had peach and drank lemonade.

Since the two other than Greg and Logan who had zucchini had French dressing (clue 10), James, Olivia, Taylor, and Zach all had asparagus.

From clue 15, neither Emma, Olivia, nor Taylor had a baked potato. From clue 18, neither did James. Therefore, only Abby can be the third drinker of fruit punch referred to in clue 6, and she had a baked potato and is the fourth and last person with balsamic vinaigrette. Since no one with a hamburger used that dressing, Cheryl had a hamburger. By elimination, Emma drank lemonade and had peach ice cream, and Abby had chocolate chip ice cream. Since the three with peach ice cream had all different dressings (clue 8), Emma did not have French dressing (as Rory did), so she used ranch dressing and by elimination Cheryl used French.

Since Greg drank sarsaparilla (clue 9), he didn't have a veggie burger. Abby and Logan, then, had veggie burgers and Greg had ribs.

Since Abby had chocolate chip and the people with baked potatoes had three different kinds of ice cream (clue 15), Cheryl, Greg, Logan, Siobhan, and Zach all had corn. Nolan and Rory had baked potatoes.

Clue 19 determines that Taylor drank iced tea and Olivia drank sarsaparilla, since Cheryl (who drank iced tea) used French dressing but no one who drank sarsaparilla did.

Since only one person with a baked potato had asparagus (clue 15), the other two had zucchini. Since they used French dressing (clue 10), they are Nolan and Rory. Everyone else except Greg and Logan had asparagus.

Puzzle 8.3: Hide and Seek

Abby took the Mount Rushmore snow globe from the library and hid it in the tool shed.

Emma took the Statue of Liberty snow globe from the sitting room and hid it in the boathouse.

Greg took the Washington Monument snow globe from the lounge and hid it in the cottage.

James took the Space Needle snow globe from the lounge and hid it in the windmill.

Logan took the Golden Gate Bridge snow globe from the sitting room and hid it in the lighthouse.

Olivia took the Alamo snow globe from the library and hid it in the old hut.

Taylor took the Gateway Arch snow globe from the sitting room and hid it in the greenhouse.

The guests and hiding places, snow globes and hiding locations, and guests and snow globes not mentioned in clues 3, 4, and 5 go together, in some combination.

From clue 6: James did not hide a snow globe in the lighthouse, take the Washington Monument snow globe, or take a snow globe from the library; the Washington Monument was not hidden in the lighthouse or taken from the library; and the snow globe hidden in the lighthouse was not from the library. James cannot have taken the Gateway Arch snow globe, since it was hidden in either the cottage, greenhouse, or lighthouse, none of which James used as a hiding place. Therefore, James took the Space Needle snow globe and hid it in either the old hut or the windmill.

By elimination, Greg and Taylor took the Gateway Arch and Washington Monument snow globes, in some combination, which means that neither of them hid a snow globe in the boathouse or tool shed. Greg and Taylor hid their snow globes in the cottage and greenhouse, in some combination, which means that neither Abby nor Emma hid theirs in one of those locations, and since Logan and Olivia didn't either (clue 3), neither of those locations can be where the Golden Gate Bridge snow globe ended up. By elimination, then, the Golden Gate Bridge snow globe was hidden in the lighthouse and was not taken by Abby or Emma.

Since the snow globes from the sitting room did not end up in the old hut or windmill (clue 7), James took the Space Needle snow globe from the lounge. Greg took the other snow globe from the lounge (clue 9). Olivia took a snow globe from the library, and Emma took one from the sitting room (clue 10).

Since Greg took either the Gateway Arch or Washington Monument, the lounge was not the location of any of the other snow globes except the Space Needle (clue 9). Since the Statue of Liberty and Gateway Arch snow globes were in the same room (clue 11), the Gateway Arch snow globe can't have been the other one that was in the lounge, so by elimination Greg took the Washington Monument from the lounge and Taylor took the Gateway Arch.

Since only Abby and Emma could have hidden a snow globe in the tool shed, Abby must have (clue 10) and that snow globe came from the library; by elimination, Emma's hiding place for the snow globe she took from the sitting room was the boathouse. Since Abby and Olivia now account for both snow globes taken from the library, by elimination Logan and Taylor took the other two snow globes from the sitting room, and those two snow globes must have been hidden in the greenhouse and lighthouse, since the other locations have been eliminated. Greg, therefore, did not hide the Washington Monument snow globe (which came from the lounge) in the greenhouse, so he hid it in the cottage, and by elimination Taylor hid the Gateway Arch snow globe in the greenhouse after taking it from the sitting room. By elimination, the snow globe that Logan took from the sitting room must have been hidden in the lighthouse, so that was the Golden Gate Bridge snow globe. The Statue of Liberty snow globe was the other one in the sitting room (clue 11), so that is the one Emma hid in the boathouse.

Since Abby did not take the Alamo snow globe (clue 8), Olivia is the one who took it from the library, and by elimination, the snow globe that Abby hid in the tool shed was Mount Rushmore. The Alamo snow globe didn't end up in the windmill (clue 8), so it was hidden in the old hut, and by elimination the Space Needle snow globe was hidden in the windmill.

Puzzle 9.1: To the Lighthouse

The killer is Greg, the only guest without a known presence in the mansion between 1 and 2 P.M. Abby is the farmer, Emma in the engineer, Greg is the diplomat, James is the cartographer, Logan is the beachcomber, and Olivia is the architect. The order in which Taylor spoke to the guests was: Olivia, Greg, Abby, James, Emma, Logan. The true statements Taylor made were to Olivia, Abby, and Emma.

Since Abby, Emma, and Olivia are the architect, engineer, and farmer, in some combination (clue 2), the other three occupations (including the beachcomber) belong to Greg, James, and Logan, in some combination. The last guest Taylor spoke to was not James or Greg, after whom Taylor spoke to Emma and Abby, respectively (clue 5). Therefore, Logan is the beachcomber and was the last person to whom Taylor spoke (clue 6).

Between 1 and 2 P.M., the beachcomber (Logan) and farmer were in their guest rooms, the architect and cartographer were in the library, and one guest was in the big game room (clue 8), leaving the whereabouts of one guest, who must be the killer, unaccounted for.

From clue 5, the sequence in which Taylor spoke to the guests includes both James/Emma and Greg/Abby in consecutive order, and from clue 7, the Greg/Abby pair must precede James/Emma. Greg and Emma's statements contradict each other, and since Taylor alternated making true and false statements (clue 15), Greg and Emma's statements must be separated by an even number of statements, so either zero or two statements are between Greg/Abby and James/Emma. Since Logan's statement was last, it's impossible for the pairs of statements to be separated by two others, and so they were consecutive, which leaves us with two possible sequences: Olivia, Greg, Abby, James, Emma, Logan; or Greg, Abby, James, Emma, Olivia, Logan.

Since James is either the cartographer or diplomat, he was not the third person to whom Taylor spoke (clue 6), so the correct order can only be Olivia, Greg, Abby, James, Emma, Logan. Since Taylor alternated statements that were true and false, either the statements to Olivia, Abby, and Emma are all true or the statements to Greg, James, and Logan are all true.

Taylor's statements to Greg, James, and Logan, if all true, would mean that Greg, having been in the library, is the cartographer, Olivia is the farmer (and was in her guest room), and the engineer was not in the big game room, which means the diplomat must have been there. The engineer would be guilty, but either Abby or Emma could be the engineer (the other would be the architect). That set of statements fails to identify a unique guilty party as promised by Nina. Therefore the other set of statements must be true.

Taylor's true statements to Abby, Emma, and Olivia mean that the engineer was in the big game room; Olivia must be the architect (she cannot be the engineer, since she was not in the big game room, per clue 4, and Taylor's statement to Emma rules her out as the farmer); and Greg was not in the library, is the diplomat, and must be the guilty party who was not in the mansion.

By elimination, James is the cartographer. Since neither Abby nor Emma is guilty, Emma is not the farmer (clue 4), which means that Abby is, and Emma is the engineer.

Puzzle 9.2: Shooting Match

Cheryl was the winner, with photos of five players (Isabel, James, Logan, Olivia, Vince).

Abby came in second, with photos of four players (Emma, Greg, Nolan, Vince).
Emma had a photo of one player (James).
Greg had photos of three players (Emma, Isabel, Vince).
Isabel had photos of three players (Abby, Logan, Taylor).
James had photos of two players (Isabel, Taylor).
Logan had photos of three players (Abby, Emma, Greg).
Nolan had photos of three players (Emma, Logan, Taylor).
Olivia had photos of two players (Abby, Greg).
Taylor had photos of three players (Abby, Olivia, Vince).
Vince had photos of two players (Isabel, Logan).

From their statements, Abby, Greg, Isabel, Logan, and Vince entered into an alliance whereby they would meet at the boathouse and pose for photos in pairs of two, so that each would come away with a photo of two players while allowing themselves to be shot by two other players. Abby took a photo of Greg and Vince (Abby's statement), and Greg took a photo of Isabel and Vince (Greg's statement). Isabel was also in Vince's photo, so the two who took photos of Isabel and Vince are now accounted for, which means Logan took a photo of Abby and Greg. By elimination, Isabel took a photo of Abby and Logan, and the other person in Vince's photo must have been Logan.

The photos taken by the alliance account for five of the nine photos showing more than one player, as enumerated by the Montagues. The photos mentioned in Logan's and Taylor's statements account for two more. Olivia's statement accounts for two more such photos, so those are the only photos taken of multiple players. Therefore, the shot of three players that Cheryl says she took must be the photo of Isabel, Logan, and Vince that Logan mentions in his statement. Olivia, per her statement, then took a photo of the other two alliance members, Abby and Greg.

Per James's statement, he took one of the photos of someone photographing another player, but Logan wasn't the photographer in James's photo, so James took the picture described by Taylor, in which someone took Taylor's photo. Nolan took the other such photo, per his statement, so he took the photo Logan described, of Logan photographing Emma. Isabel, per her statement, was shot by someone as she shot another player, so she must be the one who was shot by James in the act of taking Taylor's photo.

James and Nolan, therefore, both had photos of at least two players, and so did the five players who formed the alliance as well as Cheryl and Olivia, who took photos of three and two of the allies, respectively. Taylor stated that he took photos of Abby, Olivia, and Vince. Abby's statement that she took a photo of the player who ended up taking just one photo can therefore only refer to Emma.

For eight of the 12 photos of individual players, then, both the photo taker and subject are known:

Abby shot Emma (as explained above).
Greg shot Emma (Greg's statement).
Isabel shot Taylor (as explained above).
Logan shot Emma (Logan's statement).
Nolan shot Taylor (Nolan's statement); Taylor's statement implies that this photo is the one taken as Taylor crossed the path leading to the boathouse.
Taylor shot Abby, Olivia, and Vince (Taylor's statement); this photo of Olivia was taken near the boathouse and accounts for the photo that Olivia says was taken of her in that location, and this photo of Vince plus the group photograph including Vince taken by Cheryl accounts for the two non-allies that Vince says shot him.

Some or all of the other four photos of individual players must be in the following list of photos that can't be accounted for among the previous photos:

Abby shot the only player who was shot by no one else (Abby's statement).
Cheryl encountered someone on the path between the old well and the pond around 2:00 (Cheryl's statement).
Cheryl encountered someone near the bridge late in the game (Cheryl's statement); this was Olivia, per Olivia's statement.
Emma shot someone near the pond around 1:30 (Emma's statement).
Someone shot James near the pond before 2:00 (James's statement).
James encountered someone while walking to the old well from the pond around 2:00 (James's statement).
Olivia encountered Cheryl near the bridge late in the game (Olivia's statement).

There are two definite shooters on the list (Abby and Emma). Including Abby's as-yet-unaccounted-for photo, Abby had photos of four players, but she did not win (Abby's statement). The only player who could have ended up with more photos was Cheryl, who must have encountered James on the path between the old well and the pond and taken his picture, and then later taken Olivia's picture, making a total of five photos. Abby and Emma took the last two photos, so Emma photographed James near the pond. So far, everyone has been shot at least once except for Cheryl and Nolan. However, per Abby's statement, Abby's photo of the person only photographed by her took place no earlier than 2 P.M., and Cheryl only encountered James and Olivia from 2 P.M. on. Abby's fourth photo must therefore have been of Nolan.

Puzzle 9.3: Double Dates

James revealed that he had one N. When Emma revealed that she had two N's, her only possible date was Twenty-Four November. James's slip read Twenty-Three October. (Had Emma revealed no N's, her slip would have to have been Three October; and if she had revealed one N, her slip would have been Thirteen October. Thirty-One November could have been another possibility for two N's, if the month of November didn't have only 30 days.) James's other possible slip until revealing his single N was Fourteen November, with two N's, and so his choice of N also narrowed down his own possibilities to one for Emma, but under the rules of the game, he was the winner.

The fact that each player had a B eliminated seven months from consideration, since the B could not have come from a number. The fact that both James and Emma had two O's eliminated February, September, and December, since no number from one to thirty-one contains more than one O. Two O's can come from either an October date without an O in the number or a November date with one O. In either case, the number needs to have one R to account for the two R's on each player's slip.

To account for Emma's three E's, her slip had either an October date with a number having two E's in it or a November date with a number having one E. For James to have four E's required either an October date with a number having three E's in it or a November date with a number having two E's. Eliminating numbers without an R, October dates with an O in the number, and November dates without an O in the number reduces James's possiblites to two and Emma's to three. The only way Emma could have revealed a higher number of N's than James was if he had one and she had two.

Puzzle 10.1: Skeletons

Taylor is planning to kill James.

Abby is the litigation lawyer, has a dark secret, and knows Emma's dark secret.
Emma is the criminal lawyer and has a dark secret.
Greg is the tax lawyer and has a dark secret.
James is the corporate lawyer and knows Taylor's dark secret.
Logan is the labor lawyer and knows Emma's dark secret.
Olivia is the patent lawyer and knows Greg's dark secret.
Taylor is the estate lawyer and has a dark secret.

From Alistair's statement, Emma's specialty is not estate, litigation, or tax law (and those four all have dark secrets); likewise, from Charlotte's statement, Abby and Logan's specialties are not corporate or patent law (and those four all know dark secrets). From Evelyn's statement, the labor lawyer knows a dark secret, therefore the labor lawyer must be Abby or Logan. However, from Lyle's statement, Greg, Logan, and Taylor are the estate, labor, and tax lawyers in some order (and Abby, Emma, James, and Taylor are the other four in some order), so the labor lawyer cannot be Abby and must be Logan.

Per their statements, Abby and Logan both know Emma's dark secret. But Emma says she would never kill Abby, and per Evelyn's statement, Logan the labor lawyer is not the possible victim, so Emma is not the potential killer. Olivia and James, per their statements, are the two others who know a dark secret, so one of them must be the potential victim. Neither of them knows the litigation lawyer's secret (per Sandy) and Olivia says she doesn't know the estate lawyer's secret, so she must know the tax lawyer's secret and James knows the estate lawyer's secret. Greg and Taylor are the estate and tax lawyers in some combination, but since James says he does not know Greg's secret, Taylor must be the estate lawyer whose secret James knows, and Greg is therefore the tax attorney whose secret Olivia knows. But per Greg's statement, he would never kill Olivia, so Taylor must be the potential killer and James the potential victim.

As for everyone else's identity: Per Taylor, the patent lawyer doesn't know Taylor's secret, and since Abby is not the patent lawyer, the patent lawyer doesn't know Emma's secret either. Therefore the patent lawyer knows Greg's secret and is Olivia. The corporate lawyer also knows someone's dark secret, but since Abby is not the corporate lawyer either, the corporate lawyer must be the one who knows Taylor's dark secret, and is therefore James. By elimination, then, Abby is the litigation lawyer who has a dark secret no one knows, and Emma is the criminal lawyer.

Puzzle 10.2: Just Desserts

Abby made coconut flan and ate brownies.
Emma made cherries jubilee and ate strawberry shortcake.
Greg made vanilla soufflé and ate apple pie.
James made chocolate lava cake and ate tapioca pudding.
Logan made brownies and ate crêpes suzette.
Olivia made strawberry shortcake and ate chocolate lava cake.
Rory made apple pie and ate coconut flan.
Siobhan made tapioca pudding and ate cheesecake.
Taylor made crêpes suzette and ate vanilla soufflé.
Zach made cheesecake and ate cherries jubilee.

From clues 3 and 4, two sets of desserts were both made and eaten by the same group of five people. Abby, Greg, Logan, Rory, and Taylor were one group (who made and ate apple pie, brownies, coconut flan, crêpes suzette, and vanilla soufflé), and Emma, James, Olivia, Siobhan, and Zach were the other group (who made and ate cheesecake, cherries jubilee, chocolate lava cake, strawberry shortcake, and tapioca pudding).

From clues 10, 12, and 13, we have a partial chain of desserts, in which the person who made one eats the next in the chain: coconut flan-brownies-crêpes suzette-vanilla soufflé. If the maker of vanilla soufflé ate coconut flan, thus closing the chain, that would leave the fifth dessert in the group (apple pie) unconnected to the chain, but since no one ate his or her own dessert (per clue 2), this is impossible, so we have a closed set of five desserts: coconut flan-brownies-crêpes suzette-vanilla soufflé-apple pie (which connects back to coconut flan).

Similarly, from clues 9, 11, and 14, we get the partial chain tapioca pudding-cheesecake-cherries jubilee-strawberry shortcake. As with the other group, that chain can't close without including the fifth dessert, chocolate lava cake, so the full sequence is tapioca pudding-cheesecake-cherries jubilee-strawberry shortcake-chocolate lava cake (which connects back to tapioca pudding).

From clue 10, Greg did not make brownies. From clue 15, he did not make coconut flan, and since he didn't eat coconut flan either, he didn't make apple pie (since, per the sequence above, the maker of apple pie ate coconut flan). He also didn't make crêpes suzette (since that person ate vanilla soufflé), so Greg can only have made the vanilla soufflé. Per clue 5, Abby preceded Greg in the chain by three people, which means she made coconut flan. The chain of dessert makers, then, is Abby-?-?-Greg-?. Per clue 7, Logan ate the dessert made by Taylor, so they must be in adjacent positions in the group, with the fifth person in the other spot. That gives us the final sequence: Abby-Logan-Taylor-Greg-Rory.

A similar process resolves the other group. Clues 9 and 16 eliminate all possibilities except chocolate lava cake for the dessert made by James. Following the connections in clue 6 indicates that Zach made the cheesecake, and gives the partial chain ?-Zach-?-?-James. That chain leaves only one position for Emma and Olivia per clue 8, and Siobhan is in the remaining position, giving us Siobhan-Zach-Emma-Olivia-James. Who made and ate which dessert can now be easily determined by comparing the chains.

Puzzle 10.3: Numbers Game

Starting hands:

Abby: 15, 17, 18
Emma: 11, 16, 21
Greg: 1, 13, 19
James: 5, 8, 9
Logan: 2, 4, 6
Olivia: 3, 10, 12
Taylor: 7, 14, 20

Exchanges:

Abby and Olivia exchanged the 17 and 12.
Emma and Greg exchanged the 16 and 1.
James and Taylor exchanged the 8 and 7.

Rank of hands after the exchanges:

1. Emma: 1, 11, 21 (gaps of 10)
2. Olivia: 3, 10, 17 (gaps of 7)
3. Taylor: 8, 14, 20 (gaps of 6)
4. Greg: 13, 16, 19 (gaps of 3)
5. Abby: 12, 15, 18 (gaps of 3)
6. James: 5, 7, 9 (gaps of 2)
7. Logan: 2, 4, 6 (gaps of 2)

To have a sum of 50 (per clue 5), the three cards dealt to Abby had to be the 15, 17, and 18, since the higher-numbered cards were dealt to others (clue 2). Since Logan never traded with anyone (clue 8), he must have been one of the players who was dealt a gap straight (clue 7). Logan was dealt a 2 (per clue 1), and two of the cards he was dealt had a product of 24 (clue 6). If the 2 were part of the product, Logan's only possible gap straight would be 2-7-12, but Taylor was dealt the 7 (clue 3), so the other two cards are the ones with a product of 24; the only possibility that forms a gap straight is 2-4-6.

Olivia was dealt a 3 and two of the cards not already assigned to someone else (8, 9, 10, 11, 12, 13, 14, and 16). Per clue 8, she and Abby traded cards. For Abby to make a gap straight from her original hand, she must have traded away the 17 or 18 (since a gap of 1 isn't allowed). The possible straights she could then make from the cards Olivia might have are 12-15-18 (giving Olivia the 17) or 13-15-17 (giving Olivia the 18). But it's impossible to make a gap straight from a 3 and an 18, so Abby traded a 17 for a 12, and Olivia's other card must have been a 10 for her to end up with a gap straight of 3-10-17.

Who besides Logan began with a gap straight? Not Abby or Olivia (whose three cards are known), not James (who held a 5 and, per clues 4 and 8, traded his middle card to Taylor; possible gap straights with the available cards are 5-8-11 and 5-9-13, which could become 5-11-17 or 5-13-21, but Abby held the 17 and Emma held the 21, so he cannot have traded with Taylor for either of those cards), and not Taylor (it is impossible for a gap straight to include both 7 and 20). Greg would only have been dealt a gap straight if his third card were the 10, but Olivia was dealt the 10. Therefore, Emma was dealt a gap straight. The only one it could have been is 11-16-21, since all other possibilities that include the 21 are ruled out by other numbers' known locations.

Emma traded with Greg but still had a gap straight afterward. She can't have traded away the 11, because it's the only card that makes a gap straight with 16 and 21. If she traded the 21, she would need to receive a 6 from Greg to make the gap straight 6-11-16, but Logan holds the 6. Therefore she trades the 16 to Greg, and he gives her his 1 to make the gap straight 1-11-21. Greg's other card must be a 13 to leave him with the gap straight 13-16-19.

The only remaining cards unaccounted for in the deal are the 8, 9, and 14. As we already know from clues 2 and 3, Taylor was dealt the 7 and 20, and James was dealt the 5. From clue 4, James didn't trade away the 5 (since it's the lowest of all the cards he could possibly hold), and if he held the 14, he didn't trade that away either. But it's impossible to make a gap straight from 5 and 14, so James must have been dealt 5, 8, 9, and Taylor was dealt 7, 14, 20; they traded the 7 and 8, leaving James with 5, 7, 9 and Taylor with 8, 14, 20.

Weekend 11

Puzzle 11.1: Mini Mahjong

Greg scored 68, with pairs of 9's, 7's, and 6's and unpaired tiles with a face value of 6. $(44 + 30 - 6)$

Abby scored 67, with pairs of 9's, 8's, and 7's and unpaired tiles with a face value of 11. $(48 + 30 - 11)$

Logan scored 67, with pairs of North, East, and West winds, a pair of 1's, and unpaired tiles of the same three winds. $(2 + 40 + 25 + 0)$

Olivia scored 66, with pairs of 9's, 8's, and 7's and unpaired tiles with a face value of 12. $(48 + 30 - 12)$

Emma scored 14, with two pairs of 6's and unpaired tiles with a total face value of 30. $(24 + 20 - 30)$

James scored −3, with a pair of 8's and unpaired tiles with a total face value of 29. $(16 + 10 - 29)$

To have unpaired tiles with zero total face value (clue 2), a player's unpaired tiles must consist of all wind tiles—exactly three, since the next higher possible number of unpaired tiles is five, which would necessarily include a pair. This player must therefore be the one with four pairs, who was tied for the second-highest score (clue 1) with either Abby or Olivia (clue 5). The lowest possible score this player could have could have had is 67: 10 for each pair, 25 for having four pairs, and at least 2 points for a pair of 1's, which could be accompanied by three pairs of winds. (It's impossible to have four pairs of winds since three different players have South wind tiles, per clue 9, but also, the bonus for four pairs of wind cards would make it impossible for anyone else to earn a higher score.) Whichever player scored higher had a score of at least 68.

The winning player must have had three pairs, or would not be able to achieve a score of at least 68. (Two pairs of 9's would only be worth $36 + 20 = 56$, minus unpaired tiles.) Therefore, one player had four pairs, three players (Abby, Olivia, and the player with the best score, who wasn't Abby or Olivia per clue 5) had three pairs, one had two pairs (clue 4), and one had one pair (clue 3). The total bonus for pairs across all six scores was therefore $16 \times 10 = 160$. Subtracting this, as well as the 25-point bonus for the player with four pairs, from the total score of 279 (the result of $282 - 3$, from the information in clue 3) yields 94. Since the player with four pairs had unpaired tiles with a face value of zero, the face value of paired tiles minus the face value of unpaired tiles equals 94.

But we also know that the total face value of all 66 tiles is 270, and so the face value of paired tiles plus the face value of unpaired tiles equals 270.

Adding these equations together yields $2 \times$ (face value of paired tiles) $= 364$. So the face value of paired tiles is 182, leaving 88 as the face value of unpaired tiles. From the information in clues 4 and 6, we can now determine that the unpaired tile totals for the various players were 6, 11, 12, 29, and 30 (in addition to zero for the player with three unpaired winds). This can be done by trial and error, or algebraically by solving $0 + a + 2a + (2a - 1) + 5a + (5a - 1) = 88$, which simplifies to $15a = 90$, so that $a = 6$.

From clue 4, the players with 29 and 30 unpaired points to subtract were the players with one pair and two pairs, respectively. Since the player with one pair had a score of −3, which includes the 10 points earned for having the pair, the face value of the pair must have been 16, and so was a pair of 8s.

From clue 6, Abby and Olivia had unpaired tiles of face values 11 and 12, respectively, and the player with the highest score had unpaired tiles of value 6. Abby and Olivia's paired tiles had the same face value, so Abby's final score was one point higher than Olivia's, which means Abby must be the one who was tied for the

second-highest score with the four-pairs player, so she also scored at least 67.

From clue 7, Logan had a higher score than Emma, who had a higher score than James, and from clue 8, Logan did not have the highest score. Abby and Olivia didn't have the highest score either, so by elimination Greg had the highest score (and unpaired tiles with a face value of 6), and since only Greg had a higher score than Abby, Logan must be the player with four pairs who tied with Abby.

Greg scored at least 68, Abby and Logan scored at least 67, and Olivia scored at least 66. Taking into account their pair bonuses and leftover tiles, Greg's paired tiles had a total face value of at least 44, and Abby and Olivia's sets of paired tiles each had a combined face value of at least 48. Bearing in mind that we already know the player who scored −3 has a pair of 8's, the maximum possible face value that Greg, Abby, and Olivia's nine pairs can have is 140 (one pair of 6's, three pairs of 7's, two pairs of 8's, and three pairs of 9's). Since $44 + 48 + 48 = 140$, none of the four scored higher than their minimum possible score. Greg had no two pairs of matching denominations (clue 8), so to reach his total face value of 44 he must have had pairs of 6's, 7's, and 9's. That leaves two pairs each of 7's, 8's, and 9's for Abby and Olivia; the only way to make two sets of three pairs adding up to a face value of 48 is if they both had one pair each of 7's, 8's, and 9's.

Greg, Logan, Abby, and Olivia's scores of 68, 67, 67, and 66 add up to 268, so the player with two pairs must have scored 14 (per the total overall score in clue 3); that player was Emma (clue 7), and the sixth-place finisher with one pair was James. Taking into account the 30 points of unpaired leftover tiles in Emma's hand, the two pairs were worth 44 points, with a face value of 24 points plus 20 points pairs bonus. There are no tiles with a higher value than 6 that are still unaccounted for, so Emma must have held two pairs of 6's. That accounts for the denominations of every pair except for which three pairs of winds are held by Logan; they must be North, East, and West, since three different players hold the three South wind tiles (clue 9).

One possible distribution of the tiles is as follows (b = bamboos, c = characters, d = dots):

Greg: 9b9b 7b7b 6b6b / S 1b 1c 2b 2d
Abby: 9c9c 8c8c 7c7c / S 1c 2c 4c 4d
Logan: NN EE WW 1d1d / N E W
Olivia: 9d9d 8d8d 7d7d / 1b 2b 3b 3c 3d
Emma: 6c6c 6d6d / 3c 4c 4b 4d 5b 5c 5d
James: 8b8b / S 2c 2d 3b 3d 4b 5b 5c 5d

Puzzle 11.2: The Missing Medallion

Logan is the thief. He was in the sitting room by himself from 1:30 to 2:30, but left long enough to go to the lounge, steal the medallion, and hide it in the sitting room.

From Greg's statement, Greg and James were in the sitting room from 12:30 to 1:30; and from Alistair's statement, they were the only two in that room that hour. From her own statement, Olivia was in the dining room from 12:30 to 1:30 but then changed rooms. Per Taylor's statement, Taylor was never to have been in the dining room or library, and must have been the only person in the small game room from 12:30 to 1:30. (Why? In that hour, Greg and James were the only two in the sitting room, and the dining room and library had two guests each, per Alistair.) The two guests who were in the library from 12:30 to 1:30, as per Alistair's statement, were therefore two of Abby, Emma, and Logan; the other was in the dining room.

From 2:30 to 3:30 James was in the small game room with a guest who had been in the library from 12:30 to 1:30, per his statement. That guest was not Emma or Logan, who were in the sitting room from 2:30 to 3:30 with one other person (Emma's and Logan's statements), and so Abby was in the library from 12:30 to 1:30 and the small game room from 2:30 to 3:30. That accounts for everyone in the small game room in that hour, so by elimination Taylor was the third person in the sitting room from 2:30 to 3:30.

Emma was in the dining room from 1:30 to 2:30 (Lyle's statement), and must be the guest in Alistair's statement who did not leave the dining room at 1:30. (Olivia changed rooms after 1:30, per her statement, and whatever room Logan was in from 12:30 to 1:30, he must have changed rooms to be in the sitting room at 1:30, per his statement.) By elimination, then, Logan was in the library from 12:30 to 1:30. The guests who were in the library and sitting room from 12:30 to 1:30 all changed rooms at 1:30 (Alistair's statement). Greg was in the dining room from 1:30 to 2:30 (Sandy's statement). The only guest who could have spent two consecutive hours in the library (Charlotte's statement) is Olivia, from 1:30 to 3:30. By elimination, the three guests in the small game room from 1:30 to 2:30 (Abby's statement) were Abby, James, and Taylor. The three guests in the sitting room from 2:30 to 3:30 (Emma's statement) were Emma, Logan, and Taylor. Since Greg changed rooms at 2:30 (Sandy's statement), he was in the library after that.

In summary: From 12:30 to 1:30, Emma and Olivia were in the dining room, Abby and Logan were in the library, Greg and James were in the sitting room, and Taylor was in the small game room. From 1:30 to 2:30, Emma and Greg were in the dining room, Olivia was in the library, Logan was in the sitting room, and Abby, James, and Taylor were in the small game room. From 2:30 to 3:30, the dining room was empty, Greg and Olivia were in the library, Emma, Logan, and Taylor were in the sitting room, and Abby and James were in the small game room. From Gordon's statement, only a guest who was alone in a room had an opportunity to steal the medallion. Taylor was alone in the small game room from 12:30 to 1:30, Logan was alone in the sitting room from 1:30 to 2:30, and Olivia was alone in the library from 1:30 to 2:30.

The medallion could not have been hidden in the pantry between 12:30 and 2:30, since the dining room was occupied by two guests during that time and Evelyn was in the kitchen (Evelyn's statement). Since the medallion was not hidden in the small game room as of 1:30 (Grant's statement), Taylor could not have stolen and hidden it by that time, and Taylor was always with other guests from 1:30 until 3:30 and would have had no other opportunity to hide the medallion. Charlotte stated that the guest who was in the library from 1:30 to 3:30 never left that room, and so Olivia did not go to the lounge to steal the medallion. That leaves Logan, who had ample time to go from the sitting room to the lounge and back without being seen. He had to hide the medallion in the sitting room, since the library and small game room were occupied by others and the pantry was not accessible, as previously noted. The dining room was empty from 2:30 to 3:30, but Logan was with two other guests in the sitting room during that hour.

Puzzle 11.3: Book Exchange

Abby lent *Sixth Sense* to Greg and *Eighth Wonder* to Olivia. Emma lent *Second Fiddle* to James and *Ninth Inning* to Abby. Greg lent *Fourth Estate* to Logan and *13th Floor* to James. James lent *First Family* to Taylor and *10th Street* to Emma. Logan lent *Seventh Heaven* to Taylor and *11th Hour* to Olivia. Olivia lent *Third Degree* to Emma and *14th Amendment* to Greg. Taylor lent *Fifth Avenue* to Abby and *12th Day* to Logan.

From clues 3, 6, and 7, by elimination, *Eighth Wonder*, *Ninth Inning*, and *11th Hour* are owned by Abby, Emma, and Logan, in some combination (Greg's and Olivia's two books are one from each set in clues 6 and 7; James's are two from clues 3 and 6; and Taylor's are two from clues 3 and 7); Abby borrowed one of them and Olivia borrowed two of them (the two books borrowed by Emma and Logan are one from each set in clues 3 and 7; Greg borrowed two from clues 6 and 7; and James and Taylor borrowed two from clues 3 and 6).

From clue 4, Emma, James, Logan, and Taylor did not borrow books from Abby, and so both Greg and Olivia did. From clue 5, Emma, James, Logan, and Taylor didn't lend to Greg, so the other person he borrowed from was Olivia. (And per clue 3, Abby therefore didn't borrow from Greg or Olivia, and Olivia didn't borrow from Greg.)

Of Emma, James, Logan, and Taylor, the only exchanges within that group of four were the Emma-James and Logan-Taylor exchanges mentioned in clue 3, a book lent to someone in the group by James (clue 4), and a book borrowed by someone within the group by Taylor (clue 5). So James lent a book to Taylor, and that accounts for all the exchanges within that group.

From clue 10, James and Logan must have both borrowed from Greg, since borrowing from Olivia would mean she lent three books. By elimination, Emma borrowed from Olivia, and so Olivia did not borrow from Emma. By elimination, Abby borrowed from Emma.

Since Olivia borrowed two books from among *Eighth Wonder*, *Ninth Inning*, and *11th Hour*, which are owned by Abby, Emma, and Logan, she did not borrow from Taylor. Therefore, Olivia borrowed from Logan and Abby borrowed from Taylor.

Since Abby does not own *Second Fiddle* or *Seventh Heaven* (clue 3), she does not own *Ninth Inning* or *11th Hour* (clue 8). Since neither James nor Taylor owns *Ninth Inning* or *11th Hour*, neither of them own *Second Fiddle* or *Seventh Heaven* (clue 8).

Since Greg did not borrow *Second Fiddle*, he did not borrow *13th Floor* (clue 9). Since neither Emma nor Logan borrowed *13th Floor* (clue 6), neither of them borrowed *Second Fiddle* (clue 9). Since neither James nor Taylor borrowed *Third Degree*, neither of them borrowed *10th Street* (clue 9).

Greg borrowed books from Abby and Olivia, so one of them lent *Sixth Sense* to Greg and borrowed *Fifth Avenue* (clue 11). But Olivia didn't borrow *Fifth Avenue* (clue 7), so Abby borrowed *Fifth Avenue* and lent Greg *Sixth Sense*. Abby borrowed books from Emma and Taylor, but Emma didn't lend out *Fifth Avenue* (clue 7), so Taylor did.

Emma borrowed *10th Street* from someone who also lent out *First Family* (clue 12). The two people who lent books to Emma were James and Olivia, but Olivia didn't lend out *10th Street* (clue 3), so James did, and therefore the book that James lent to Taylor was *First Family*. Since we've already determined that Taylor doesn't own *Second Fiddle* or *Seventh Heaven*, by elimination the other book that Taylor lent out (to Logan) was *12th Day*, per clue 3.

Since Logan did not lend *Second Fiddle* or *Ninth Inning* (clue 13), Emma owned *Second Fiddle* and *Ninth Inning* and Logan owned *Seventh Heaven* and *11th Hour*. Since Emma lent books to Abby and James but Abby did not borrow *Second Fiddle* (clue 3), James borrowed it, and Emma lent *Ninth Inning* to Abby. We've already shown that of *Eighth Wonder*, *Ninth Inning*, and *11th Hour*, one was lent to Abby and two to Olivia, so Olivia borrowed *Eighth Wonder* and *11th Hour*. Logan owned *11th Hour*, so *Eighth Wonder* must be the book Olivia borrowed from Abby. The other book lent out by Logan was borrowed by Taylor, so Taylor borrowed *Seventh Heaven*.

All the books borrowed by Abby, Olivia, and Taylor are accounted for. By elimination, James borrowed *13th Floor* and Greg borrowed *14th Amendment*. Greg didn't borrow from himself, obviously, so he borrowed *14th Amendment* from Olivia and James borrowed *13th Floor* from Greg.

The last remaining books are *Third Degree* and *Fourth Estate*, which are in some order the book that Greg lent Logan, and the book that Olivia lent Emma. Olivia did not lend *Fourth Estate* (clue 13), so she lent Emma *Third Degree*, and Greg lent *Fourth Estate* to Logan.

Weekend 12

Puzzle 12.1: Attack in the Foyer

The attempted murderer is Emma, whose statement is demonstrably false.

Abby is the glazier and has jealousy for a motive.
Emma is the naturalist and has anger for a motive.
Greg is the illustrator and has greed for a motive.
James is the herpetologist and has revenge for a motive.
Logan is the machinist and has fear for a motive.
Olivia is the jeweler and has blackmail for a motive.
Taylor is the librarian and has insanity for a motive.

The statements by Alistair, Charlotte, and Evelyn eliminate about half of the possible combinations of guest and occupation, guest and motive, and occupation and motive. The four guests, occupations, or motives not mentioned by each of these staff members go together in some combination.

Neither Emma nor Logan can be the glazier or illustrator, since guests with those occupations do not have anger, fear, or revenge as a possible motive, and for the same reason James cannot be the librarian. Since that leaves both machinist and naturalist as the only possible occupations for Emma and Logan, they must have those occupations in some combination. Neither Abby nor Greg, therefore, is the machinist or naturalist. Since neither Emma nor Logan can have blackmail as their motive, neither the machinist nor naturalist can.

Abby and Greg must be the glazier and illustrator, in some combination, and since blackmail is not a possible motive for those occupations, it is not the motive of either Abby or Greg. Taylor's possible motive isn't blackmail either (Sandy's statement), so by elimination, Olivia's possible motive is blackmail, which means she cannot be the librarian, and by elimination Taylor must be.

Since neither the machinist nor the naturalist had revenge as a motive (Grant's and Lyle's statements), Emma and Logan do not have that motive, so by elimination, James's motive is revenge. Emma and Logan's motives are anger and fear, in some combination, so the herpetologist and jeweler do not have either of these motives. Emma's and Logan's statements about their own motives cannot both be true (if Emma's motive is anger, her statement is false; if Logan's motive is anger, his statement is false), so one of them is guilty. Therefore the statements made by the other five guests are trustworthy.

Per Abby's true statement, the jeweler's motive isn't revenge and is therefore blackmail, so the herpetologist's motive is revenge; James, then, is the herpetologist and Olivia is the jeweler. Per Olivia's true statement, Abby isn't the illustrator and must be the glazier (and by elimination, Greg is the illustrator), and since neither Abby nor the illustrator were motivated by insanity, Taylor the librarian was. Per Greg's true statement, Greg was not

motivated by jealousy, so his motive was greed and Abby's was jealousy. Per Taylor's true statement, Logan isn't the naturalist, so Logan is the machinist and Emma is the naturalist. And per James's true statement, the naturalist's motive isn't fear, so Logan's motive is fear and Emma's is anger. Emma's statement is false, and she is the guilty party.

Puzzle 12.2: Tropical Taste Test

All seven guests identified mango and papaya. In addition:
Abby identified guava, for a score of 3.
Emma identified cherimoya, guava, passion fruit, persimmon, and star fruit, for a score of 7.
Greg identified dragon fruit, guava, passion fruit, and persimmon, for a score of 6.
James identified cherimoya, persimmon, and star fruit, for a score of 5.
Logan identified nothing else, for a score of 2.
Olivia identified every fruit except rambutan, for a score of 9.
Taylor identified every fruit except cherimoya and lychee, for a score of 8.

Cherimoya and dragon fruit each scored 3, guava 5, lychee 1, mango and papaya 7 each, passion fruit 4, persimmon 5, rambutan 1, and star fruit 4.

Since no guest identified 10 fruits (clue 4) and no two guests had the same number correct (clue 2), the greatest possible total of correct identifications guests could have made was 42, if the combination of guesses were 9-8-7-6-5-4-3. Since the actual total was 40 (clue 1), these numbers need to be reduced by a total of 2, and the only combinations that do this while keeping all the numbers different are 9-8-7-6-5-4-1 and 9-8-7-6-5-3-2.

Since two fruits were identified by all seven guests (clue 3), the other eight fruits must account for the other 26 identifications. Since the total identifications for the fruits all came in pairs of matching numbers (clue 3), there need to be four different numbers greater than 0 but less than 7 that add up to 13, each of which will have been the number of times that two different fruits were identified. The possibilities are 1-2-4-6 and 1-3-4-5. If the least successful guest only named one fruit correctly, neither of these possible fruit score combinations would be consistent with clue 5. Therefore, the least successful guest identified two fruits, the guests had correct totals of 9-8-7-6-5-3-2, and the fruits were identified by 1-1-3-3-4-4-5-5-7-7 guests.

Since Taylor's score is two more than double Abby's (clue 6), it must either be 6 (if Abby's score is 2) or 8 (if Abby's score is 3). Since Abby scored higher than Logan (clue 7), Logan's score is 2, Abby's is 3, and Taylor's is 8. From clue 9, Olivia's score is 9.

Lychee and rambutan scored 1 each, since Olivia and Taylor both identified every other fruit except cherimoya, which was also identified by Emma and James (clue 10).

From clues 11 and 12, mango and papaya must each have scored 7, and the other fruits mentioned all scored 3 or 4. Therefore, guava and persimmon had the scores of 5, and so did James (clue 8). Mango and papaya are the only fruits that Logan identified.

From clue 13, Greg identified persimmon but not star fruit, and everyone else either identified or failed to identify both, so persimmon's score was one more than star fruit's, which means star fruit scored 4. From clue 14, cherimoya and dragon fruit had to each have a score of 3, leaving passion fruit with the other score of 4. Abby only identified one fruit besides mango and papaya, so she can't have identified persimmon or star fruit, and so Emma and

James must have identified both. All five fruits identified by James are now accounted for, so he didn't identify any others.

Since cherimoya scored 3, it was not identified by Abby or Greg. Since Greg scored 6 or 7 (the only scores not yet known) but failed to identify cherimoya, lychee, rambutan, and star fruit, he must have identified all the remaining fruits for a score of 6. Emma's score is therefore 7.

The dragon fruit was identified by Greg, Olivia and Taylor, and therefore by no one else. With its score of 5, guava was identified by Abby and Emma (as well as Greg, Olivia, and Taylor). Since Abby's score was 3, she did not identify passion fruit, but Emma did to reach her score of 7.

Puzzle 12.3: Revelation

Cheryl's statements are the only set of three that can all be true. Most of the statements are interconnected and can be chained together such that some must be true and the rest false, or vice versa.

For instance, if Cheryl's first statement is true, Siobhan's third statement is false, Isabel's second statement is true, Cheryl's third statement is true, Rory's second statement is true, Isabel's third statement is false, Rory's first statement is false, and so on. Finding every connection between statements will determine a unique set of true-false values for each statement, most of which are dependent on whether we assume the first statement to be true or false. (As it happens, three statements are the same no matter what: Isabel's first statement and Siobhan's second statement must be true, and Vince's first statement must be false.) The two possibilities for every statement's truth value are shown in the two right-hand columns of the following table.

Cheryl	1	T	F
	2	T	F
	3	T	F
Isabel	1	T	T
	2	T	F
	3	F	T
Vince	1	F	F
	2	F	T
	3	F	T
Rory	1	F	T
	2	T	F
	3	F	T
Siobhan	1	T	F
	2	T	T
	3	F	T
Zach	1	T	F
	2	F	T
	3	F	T

Only Cheryl's statements can possibly all be true.

Epilogue

Cheryl is Gordon Montague's granddaughter. As he explained to Taylor between weekends 9 and 10, Gordon was married briefly to a young woman named Margaret when he was in college. His bride's family soon insisted that the marriage be annulled, and, after many anguished scenes, succeeded in convincing their daughter to go with them to South America, where the family maintained a home. Gordon was unable to stay in touch with her. When he finally had the resources to search for her a few years later, he learned that she had died in a car accident.

What he didn't know is that she had had a child, his child, a daughter who was raised by her maternal grandparents. At 17, that daughter married and gave birth to Cheryl a year later.

Cheryl's mother's grandparents had never wanted Cheryl to have contact with Gordon, but before they passed away, they finally told Cheryl's mother about the father she had never met. That was six months ago.

Cheryl, 21, had graduated from college the previous December, a full semester early, and had several months free before entering law school in the fall. And so, when her mother told her about Gordon, the two of them resolved that instead of just showing up and announcing who they were, Cheryl would try to get to know him before deciding whether they should become part of his life.

Cheryl's research led her to Taylor, who she learned had once solved a theft problem for the Montagues. She flew from California to meet with Taylor, who verified her story and agreed to help her find a way to visit the island incognita. Taylor contacted Nolan, and the two of them came up with the idea of Cheryl being Nolan's guest in the island cottage a few times. As things turned out, the two of them are now dating.

Cheryl wanted to gradually prepare Gordon for her revelation by presenting clues that would start him thinking about his past. It was Taylor who buried the artifacts near the old well and created the mosaic code. Over the course of the summer, Taylor tried to ensure that Cheryl and Gordon spent time together, subtly suggesting several times to the Montagues that Cheryl be included in some of their games and puzzles.

Taylor helped Cheryl decide when the message leading to the ceramic pot would be sent and informed her of Gordon's reaction to it. Taylor tried to persuade Cheryl to tell Gordon her secret sooner, but Cheryl remained intent on waiting until the other guests had left for the season.

Taylor also took responsibility for telling Nina everything a week ago, and Nina had reacted as Taylor had hoped, thrilled for Gordon while agreeing to keep the secret a bit longer.

"Gordon," Taylor began, "Meet your granddaughter." Then Taylor explained everything.

"Shall I call you grandpa?" Cheryl asked with a smile. "By the way, my mother—the daughter you've never met—says hello, and plans to be on the next plane, along with my father and my younger brother."

Gordon was speechless. And there were hugs and tears all around.